ASE MANUAL DRIVE TRAIN AND AXELS (UNIT III)

Remember to:

Ask for help when needed

Use the CD resources

Take your time

Keep your textbook safe

When this ASE unit is complete, you should have:

Completed all the bullet points (your instructor may help with this task)

Labeled all the diagrams (use the CD to do this)

Completed all the knowledge checks (KCs)

Made notes and any key points in the blank spaces

Completed all the worksheets specified by your instructor

Scored 70% or more in each module test

CONTENTS

Acknowledgments

The author is grateful to the following companies for supplying assistance and/or material to help with the production of this textbook and its associated CDs. Please note that the material supplied in the textbook and on CD is for educational use only.

Alpine	Lucas
AP Racing	Mazda
Beru	Michelin
Chrysler	Phillips
Colchester Institute	Robert Bosch
Eberspacher	Snap-on Tools
Essex Radiators	T&M Auto-electrical Co.
Ford Care Institute	Thurrock College
Ford Motor Company	Triggs Garage
General Motors	VDO Instruments
Gosnays Engineering	Volvo
Jaguar	

Picture Credits

Front cover image courtesy of Ford Motor Company and Wieck Media Services, Inc. Thanks are also due to the following sources for permission to reproduce pictures:

1. Ford Motor Company
2. Ford Motor Company and Wieck Media Services, Inc.
3. Bosch GmbH
4. Photo Bosch
5. Snap-on Tools

(Number references, as above, are printed as superscripts at the end of the picture captions where necessary.)

Foreword

This has been a very exciting automotive project to work on. To date I have published several automotive textbooks but this new series is special. I got to work with a great team of people at DigitalUP; without their enthusiasm and hard work you would not be reading this now! A special thank you to them - it is well deserved.

The best part for me, about this project, is that the combination of materials (textbook, CD, worksheets, etc.) means learning about automobiles is not only more fun, it is also possible to work smarter – not just harder. I have worked in the automotive trade all my life and I still enjoy learning new things. I hope you enjoy your career as much as I have, and still do today. Remember, the key thing about this product is that it is a CD with a textbook attached – not the other way around. Enjoy!

Comments from instructors and students alike are welcomed; just follow the web link on the CD.

Good luck with your studies and career.

Tom Denton, Senior Author, DigitalUP

OK, so where do I start?

First, make sure you have the CD that comes with this textbook – these are your two key resources. Many books come with a CD in the back; however, this CD is so comprehensive – it has a textbook attached!

Second, the CD runs right from the drive of a PC, so try it out now; you can't do any harm. Click the help button for a quick description of how it works – or try the many different features anyway; it's very easy to use.

Read through this short 'getting started' guide before you start working.

When you see this 'flag' in the textbook, look at the CD for a better picture, animation, or video.

Script like this is used to represent what you may choose to write in your textbook

Why is this book different from other textbooks?

Each 'row' represents one 'screen' of learning on the CD. These are bite-sized chunks that are easy to learn. Concentrate on one part before you move on and build up your skills step by step.

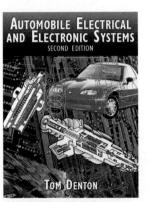

AUTOMOBILE ELECTRICAL AND ELECTRONIC SYSTEMS
SECOND EDITION

TOM DENTON

'Normal' textbook – a very good one!

What's a knowledge check?

This is a question used to check knowledge! Complete the knowledge checks (KCs) at the end of each section in the textbook and any other instructor set assignments. This allows you to assess your own progress. It's normal to go over things several times so don't expect to get everything right the first time.

KC

Explain why completing labels is a good exercise

Your answer: This helps me to remember the names of important components

Why are labels not included on the textbook diagrams?

You should add labels to the diagrams and, where necessary, copy other simple diagrams from the CD into your textbook. This will help you remember the names of important components. It is also a good way to learn how systems work.

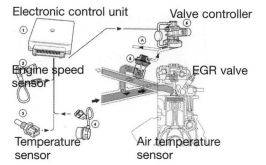

Electronic control unit   Valve controller

Engine speed sensor   EGR valve

Temperature sensor   Air temperature sensor

The screen that corresponds to this, and similar, diagrams on the CD has all the labels completed – just copy them in

Notes:
Add comments anytime you like! For example:

Component number 6 controls the flow as determined by the ECU (number 1)

How do I know what 'bullet points' to write into the textbook?

You should write anything that is useful to you in your textbook. However, your instructor will probably suggest some key points to include as 'bullets.' Remember, this is your book; any extra notes or diagrams are to help you, not others, so color in pictures, make sketches, or add anything that helps you learn.

Suggestions for bullets about the getting started guide
- *Writing key points down helps us to remember*
- *Using different methods makes learning easier*
- *Coloring in important parts of a diagram helps to show important aspects*
- *Make good use of the glossary*

What is Blended Learning?

This system is known as 'blended learning' because it includes several components that are used together. It's a complete learning system and you can learn in your own time as necessary. However, it works best with extra input from an instructor. The package uses different ways of explaining the same thing a number of times – this is a good way to learn. Learning from a computer screen is great – but it doesn't completely replace other equally good methods!

Blended learning means using different methods to their best advantage

Why is the material in topics, modules, and sections?

This is mostly to split the complexity of a modern car into manageable learning sections. Each of the eight ASE units, presented as separate books and CDs, has a number of topics, which in turn have modules and sections. Some of the sections are similar across different units. This is because some users may start their study in different places. Some of the guidance about tools, health and safety, and diagnostics is also repeated. However, the sections are not identical, so take care not to miss anything!

It is recommended that just one section is studied at any one time.

Structure of the material

ASE Unit
Topic 1.
    Module 1. Technology
      Section 1, 2 and 3
    Module 2. Technology
      Section 1, 2 and 3
    Module 3. Maintenance Operations
      Section 1. Health and Safety
      Section 2. Service/Routine Maintenance
      Section 3. Customer Care
    Module 4. Checking System Performance
      Section 1. Checking the System
      Section 2. Test Equipment
      Section 3. Faultfinding and Inspections
    Module 5. Component Inspection and Repair
      Section 1. Tools & Equipment
      Section 2. Remove & Refit/Strip & Rebuild Components
      Section 3. Inspect/Measure Components
Topic 2.
Etc.

Why do some sections appear to be missing?

In some books, not all the sections within a topic area are included because they are not relevant to that particular ASE unit.

Just part of some topics included in the material

ASE Unit
Topic 3 (part)
    Module 1. Technology
      Section 3
    Module 5. Component Inspection and Repair
      Section 3. Inspect/Measure Components

What are the main parts I will use?

In addition to this textbook, the main components of 'Automotive Technology: The Electronic Classroom' that you will use are the:
- Training CD
- Glossary
- Multiple choice questions
- Practical worksheets

Your instructor also has access to some other great resources

The CD interface is very easy to use

Glossary

Question screen

Practical worksheet

What's so special about the Automotive Training CD?

The Automotive Training CD is the heart of the Electronic Classroom. A typical screen is shown here. Note that every learning screen has a voiceover and the text can be shown. The CD contains the worksheets and hundreds of multiple choice questions. It also has lots of other features and ways of accessing the learning material. Remember, the CD has this book attached – not the other way around!

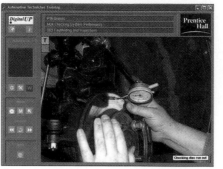

An example from the program

Where do I find the glossary?

A comprehensive automotive glossary can be accessed at any time from the main CD program. It is also displayed when a link in the Reference box is clicked. The glossary is easy to use. Just selecting the letter from the tabs and then clicking a word will show a simple definition. We've done our best, but if you find a word missing – email and let me know!

Translations into other languages, including Spanish, are included for most entries.

'F' in glossary window!

Where do I find the multiple choice questions?

A large number of multiple choice questions are built into the CD program. You should aim to score 100% in all tests but if not, then at least 70%! The questions are based on ASE test example questions. At all levels in the main access menus, a 'Questions for these Options' hyperlink appears. Click this link at any time to jump to the question screens. The number of questions available changes depending on where you are in the menu structure. For example, if you are inside a module, then there are about fifteen questions available specific to the content of the module. If you are at the top end of the menu structure, then many more questions can be accessed, but of course they are less specific.

This screen allows you to choose how many questions to do for the computer- based test – or instructors can print if required.

The question screens include a timer that allows a maximum of 60 seconds for each question. Click the 'correct' hyperlink to move on.

What's a question review screen?

One of the most powerful parts of the CD program is its ability to review questions that you answered incorrectly – and direct you back to an appropriate part of the learning material. If the Link button is followed then use the Return button to get back to the review screen. At this point you can move backward and forward through any incorrectly answered questions. Do multiple choice tests regularly; it's a good way to focus on what you need to learn.

Question review screens appear if you get any wrong!

Do I have to do all the practical worksheets?

Practical worksheets are supplied to cover all requirements of the ASE standards. The worksheets can be accessed from the main learning program on the CD. The tasks on the worksheets range from simple things like changing a fuse to advanced faultfinding. A section is included to allow you to add comments after the task has been completed. The worksheets should only be used under supervision. You don't need to do all of them, but the more the better!

Worksheet

I'm getting the idea now, but how do all the pieces work together?

The simple process here is one suggestion as to how you can use the material. However, the best way is exactly as your instructor says!

1. Read a workbook section
2. Work through the same section on the CD
3. Complete any missing labels and add key bullet points
4. Carry out the Knowledge Checks in the textbook and any activities on the CD
5. Recap as required if your answers were not correct
6. Complete appropriate worksheets in the practical sections (modules 3, 4 and 5)
7. Repeat as above on the next section (modules usually have 3 sections)
8. Carry out a multiple choice test/quiz when a module is complete
9. Work carefully through any review screens
10. Do the test again until you are, or your instructor is, satisfied with the result!

Finally?

I hope you enjoy using Automotive Technology: The Electronic Classroom as much as we have enjoyed producing it.

Good luck with your studies. Keep in touch.

We have ignition...[4]

Main Automotive Learning Program Features

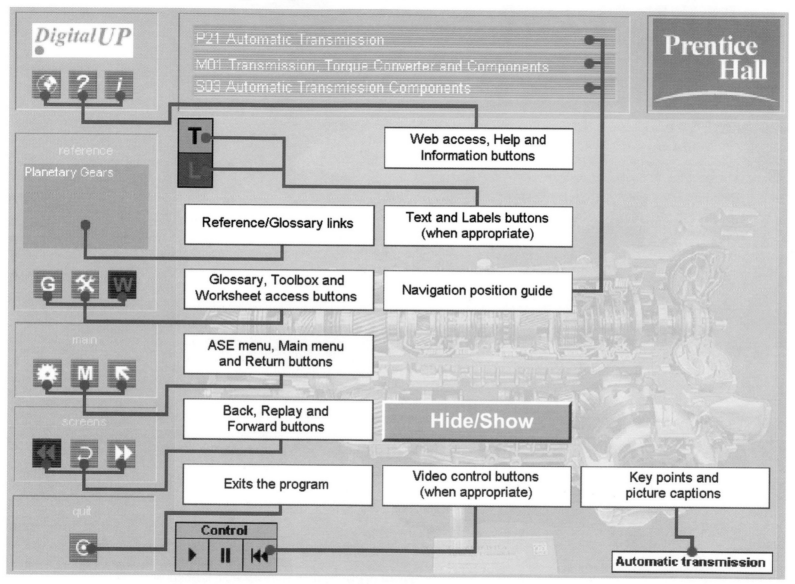

ASE Units, Topics, Modules, and Sections

Engine Repair

Engine Mechanical
Module 1. Operating Cycles and Components
Introduction
Operating Cycles
Engine Components
Engine Operating Details
Engine Terminology and Systems
Module 2. Variations In Engine Design
Cylinder Components
Valves and Valve Gear
Engine Layouts and Designs
Engine Variations
Engine Lubrication
Module 1. Lubrication System
Friction and Lubrication
Lubrication System Operation
Module 2. Lubrication Components
Oil Pumps and Filtration
Other Lubrication Components
Engine Cooling And In-Car Heating
Module 1. Cooling System Operation
Introduction
System Requirements
Components and Operation
Module 2. Cooling and Heating System Components
Introduction
Antifreeze
Engine Design Components
Heater and Temperature Gauge

Engine Performance

Engine Mechanical (part)
Module 1. Operating Cycles and Components
Introduction
Operating Cycles
Parts of modules 3, 4 and 5
Engine Lubrication (part)
Parts of modules 3 and 4
Ignition Systems
Module 1. Conventional Ignition
Introduction
Electronics and System Operation
Dwell and Timing Components
Module 2. Electronic and Programmed Ignition
Electronic Systems
Ignition Module and ECU
Engine Management
Spark Plugs and Secondary Circuit
Systems in Use
Fuel Systems
Module 1. Gasoline Fuel Systems
Carburetors
Mechanical Fuel Injection
Electronic Fuel Injection Systems
New System – Bosch DI-Motronic
Air Supply, Exhaust Systems and Emission Control
Module 1. Air Supply Systems
Air Pollution from Motor Vehicles Systems
Development for Environmental Protection
Air Supply System and Intake
Air Temperature Control Mechanism
Module 2. Exhaust and Emission Control Systems
Exhaust Systems
Catalyst Systems
Emission Control Systems
Turbocharging and Supercharging
Engine Cooling And In-Car Heating (part)
Module 1. Cooling System Operation
Components and Operation
Parts of modules 3, 4 and 5

Electrical/Electronic Systems

Battery, Charging And Starting Systems
Module 1. Batteries
Introduction and Battery Construction
Battery Capacity and State Of Charge
Battery Types and Charging
Module 2. Starting and Charging
Starting System
Charging System
Electrical/Electronic Principles
Module 1. Introduction to Electricity
Electricity and the Atom
Basic Electrical Circuits and Components
Vehicle Electrical Circuits
Module 2. Introduction to Electronics
Electronic Components
Digital Systems
Instrumentation
Module 1. Instrumentation and Sensors
Sensors
Gauges
A Digital Instrumentation System
Module 2. Driver Warning Systems
Vehicle Condition Monitoring and Trip Computers
Instrument Displays
New Developments
Lighting and Indicators
Module 1. Exterior Lighting
Lighting Systems
Lighting Circuits
New Lighting Technology
Module 2. Signaling and Interior Lighting
Indicators and Hazard Lights
Stoplights and Reverse Lights
Interior Lighting
Body Electrical/Electronic Systems
Module 1. Electrical and Electronic Systems
Introduction and Audible Warnings
Central Locking
Manual and Electric Window Operation
Module 2. Mobile Multimedia, Security and Safety Systems
Heated Glass and Mirrors
Washers and Wipers
Comfort and Security Systems

Manual Drive Train and Axles

Manual Transmission Clutch
Module 1. Clutch Introduction
Transmission System Overview
Purpose of the Clutch Components
Clutch Operating Mechanisms
Module 2. Clutch Components
Diaphragm Clutch
Coil Spring Clutch
Other Types of Clutch
Manual Transmission Gearbox
Module 1. Manual Transmission Principles
Transmission System Overview
Purpose of the Gearbox
Gears and Components
Module 2. Front and Rear Wheel Drive Transmission
Gear Change Mechanisms
Synchromesh Mechanism
Front and Rear Wheel Drive Gearboxes
Transmission Driveline
Module 1. Transmission Driveshafts
Transmission Propshafts
Driveshafts
Module 2. Wheel Bearings and Layouts
Rear Wheel Drive Bearings
Front Wheel Drive Bearings
Four-Wheel Drive Systems
Manual Transmission Final Drive and Differential
Module 1. Transmission Final Drive
Introduction to Transmission
Final Drive
Traction Control
Module 2. Differentials
Differential Operation
Limited Slip Differentials
Other Differentials and Units

Suspension and Steering

Steering Systems
Module 1. Steering Systems
Introduction to Steering
Steering Geometry
Steering Racks and Boxes
Module 1. Power Steering Systems
Introduction to Power Steering
Hydraulic Power Steering
Electric Power Steering
Suspension Systems
Module 1. Principles of Suspension
Reasons for Suspension
Springs
Dampers/Shock Absorbers
Module 2. Suspension Systems
Front Suspension Layouts
Rear Suspension Layouts
Electronically Controlled Suspension
Wheels and Tires
Module 1. Wheels
Types of Wheel
Wheel Rims and Fixings
Wheel Balancing
Module 2. Tires
Introduction
Tire Construction
Functions of the Tire

Brakes

Brakes
Module 1. Braking Components
Introduction
Hydraulic Components
Disc, Drum and Parking Brakes
Module 2. Servos, Force Control and ABS
Brake Servo Operation
Braking Force Control
Antilock Bake Systems
Manual Transmission Driveline (part)
Module 2. Wheel Bearings and Layouts
Rear Wheel Drive Bearings
Front Wheel Drive Bearings
Manual Transmission Final Drive and Differential (part)
Module 1. Transmission Final Drive
Traction Control
Lighting and Indicators (part)
Module 2. Signaling and Interior
Stoplights and Reverse Lights

Heating & Air Conditioning

Heating And Air Conditioning
Module 1. Vehicle Heating and Ventilation
Ventilation Systems
Vehicle Heating
Other Heating Systems
Module 2. Air Conditioning
Air Conditioning Fundamentals
Air Conditioning Components
Air Conditioning Systems
Engine Cooling And In-Car Heating
Module 1. Cooling System Operation
Introduction
System Requirements
Components and Operation
Module 2. Cooling and Heating System Components
Introduction
Antifreeze
Engine Design Components
Heater and Temperature Gauge

Automatic Transmission/Transaxle

Automatic Transmission
Module 1. Transmission, Torque Converter and Components
Transmission Overview
Torque Converter
Transmission Components
Module 2. Transmission Control and Case Studies
Hydraulic Control
Electronic Control
Constantly Variable Systems
Transmission Driveline
Module 1. Transmission Driveshafts
Transmission Propshafts
Driveshafts
Module 2. Wheel Bearings and Layouts
Rear Wheel Drive Bearings
Front Wheel Drive Bearings
Four-Wheel Drive Systems

Science (CD only)

Introductory Science
Module 1. Units, Sound and Atomic Structure
S.I. Units
Atoms and Molecules
Sound Waves
Module 2. Forces and Center of Gravity
Force and Pressure
Center of Gravity
Module 3. Mechanical Advantage and Energy
Machines - Mechanical Advantage
Conservation of Energy
Module 4. Electricity, Magnetism and Light
Electricity and Magnetism
Electromagnetic Waves and Light
Module 5. Temperature, Heat and Gas Laws
Heat and Temperature
Thermal Expansion and Change of State - Solid, Liquid and Gas
Gas Laws - Pressure, Temperature and Volume

Practical Modules

The following modules and sections are common to all topics except science:
Module 3. Maintenance Operations
Health and Safety
Service/Routine Maintenance
Customer Care
Module 4. Checking System Performance
Checking the System
Test Equipment
Faultfinding and Inspections
Module 5. Component Inspection and Repair
Tools & Equipment
Remove & Refit/Strip & Rebuild Components
Inspect/Measure Components

TOPIC: MANUAL TRANSMISSION CLUTCH

Module 1. Clutch Introduction
Section 1. Transmission System Overview

Introduction

Transmission is a general term used to describe all of the components required to transmit power from the engine to the wheels. The requirement is to convert the power from the relatively high velocity and low torque of the engine crankshaft, to the variable, usually lower speed and higher torque needed at the wheels.

Transmission components are vital[2]

Types of Transmission

The two basic types of transmissions use either a manual gearbox, in which the gears are selected by the driver, or an automatic gearbox, in which the gears are changed automatically.

Manual transmission

Automatic transmission

Front-Wheel Drive Transmission

Working from the engine to the wheels, the main components of a typical front-wheel drive transmission system are as follows:

Clutch

Gearbox

Final drive

Differential

Driveshafts.

Clutch

Gearbox

Final drive and differential

Driveshaft

Rear-Wheel Drive Transmission

Working from the engine to the wheels, the main components of a typical rear-wheel drive transmission system are as follows:

Clutch

Gearbox

Propshaft

Final drive

Differential

Half shafts

Clutch   Gearbox   Propshaft   Final drive and differential

Clutch

Fitted between the engine and gearbox, the clutch allows the drive to be disconnected when the pedal is depressed. It allows a smooth take-up of drive and allows gears to be changed.

Clutch assembly

Manual Gearbox

A manual gearbox is a box full of gears of varying ratios. The ratio most suitable for the current driving conditions can be selected by the gearshift. Most boxes contain about thirteen gear cogs, which allow five forward gears and one reverse.

A box of gears!

Torque Converter

A torque converter is sometimes called a fluid flywheel (although the two differ slightly) and is used in conjunction with an automatic gearbox. It has two main parts. As the input section rotates, fluid pressure begins to act on the output section, which is made to rotate. As speed increases, a better drive is made. Therefore, the drive takes up automatically and smoothly.

Fluid clutch and torque converter

Automatic Gearbox

As the name suggests, this is a gearbox that operates automatically. Most types contain special gear arrangements, known as epicyclic gear trains. Some now use very complicated electronic control, but the basic principle is that fluid pressure from a pump, which changes with road speed, is used to change the gears.

Epicyclic gears are often used in an 'auto-box'

Final Drive

To produce the required torque at the road wheels, a fixed-gear reduction from the high engine speed is required. The final drive consists of just two gears with a ratio of about 4:1. These are bevel gears on rear-wheel drive systems and normal gears on front-wheel drive systems.

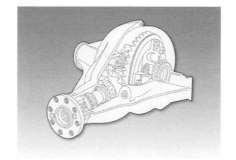

Differential and final drive combination

Differential

A special combination of gears allows the driven wheels of a vehicle to rotate at different speeds. Think of a car going around a bend: The outer wheel has to travel a greater distance, and hence must rotate at a faster speed than the inner wheel. If this was not allowed to happen, the drive would "wind up" and something would break.

The differential can be called a torque equalizer

Driveshafts

Two driveshafts are used to pass the drive from the outputs of the final drive to each wheel. Each driveshaft contains two constant velocity joints. These joints are covered with a rubber boot to keep out water and dirt.

This shaft transmits drive to the wheels

Propshaft

On rear-wheel drive vehicles, the drive has to be passed from the gearbox output to the final drive and differential unit in the rear axle. The propshaft, short for propeller shaft, is a hollow tube with a universal joint at each end. If removed, the universal joints must be realigned correctly.

This shaft transmits drive to the final drive

Universal Joint

The universal joint (UJ) is like a cross with a bearing on each leg. It allows drive to be transmitted through an angle. This is to allow for suspension movement.

This is called a UJ

Constant Velocity Joint

The constant velocity joint (CV) is a bit like a universal joint. It is used on front-wheel drive driveshafts. It allows a smooth, constant velocity drive to be passed through, even when the suspension moves up and down and the steering moves side to side.

CV joints allow for this movement

Summary

The clutch is a key component in the transmission system. However, it works in conjunction with other parts. All should be operating correctly for optimum performance.

The clutch is a key component[2]

Read the last few pages again and note down FIVE bullet points here:

KC   Explain the purpose of a propshaft.

Notes

Purpose of the Clutch

A clutch is a device for disconnecting and connecting rotating shafts. In a vehicle with a manual gearbox, the driver depresses the clutch when changing gear, thus disconnecting the engine from the gearbox. It allows a temporary neutral position for gear changes and also a gradual way of taking up drive from rest.

Operation of the clutch pedal

Automatic Transmission

Cars with automatic transmissions do not have clutches as described here. Drive is transmitted from the flywheel to the automatic gearbox by a torque converter, sometimes called a fluid clutch.

Torque converter components

Gearbox

For most light vehicles, a gearbox has five forward gears and one reverse gear. It is used to allow operation of the vehicle through a suitable range of speeds and torque. A manual gearbox needs a clutch to disconnect the engine crankshaft from the gearbox while changing gears. The driver changes gears by moving a gearshift, which is connected to the box by a mechanical link.

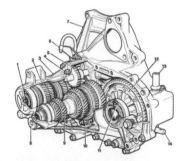

Internal view of a gearbox[1]

Clutch Components

Each of the following screens covers one or more typical clutch components. Some are more important than others. The driven plate and the pressure plate are the two main parts.

Driven plate and pressure plate

Reluctor Ring

In conjunction with a sensor, the reluctor ring provides a signal for the ignition and fuel systems. It supplies information on engine speed and position. However, it is not part of the clutch!

Supplies signals
(click to zoom in/out)

Flywheel

The flywheel keeps the engine running smoothly between power strokes. It also acts as a surface against which the driven plate can press. A locking plate is used for security of the flywheel.

The flywheel is part of the clutch (click to zoom in/out)

Driven Plate

The driven plate is a friction material plate, which is clamped between the pressure plate and the flywheel. It is splined onto the gearbox input shaft. The small coil springs are to prevent the clutch from snatching as drive is taken up.

A friction material plate (click to zoom in/out)

Pressure Plate

This cover of the pressure plate is fixed to the flywheel with a ring of bolts. The fingers in the center act as springs and levers to release the pressure. Drive is transmitted unless the fingers are pressed in toward the flywheel.

The fingers in the center act as springs (click to zoom in/out)

Release Bearing

A release shaft transfers the movement of the cable to the release fork and bearing. The bearing pushes against the clutch fingers when the pedal is depressed and releases the drive. A return spring is used so that when the clutch pedal is not depressed, the bearing allows the clutch fingers to return outward. A seal is fitted to keep out water and dirt.

The bearing pushes against the clutch fingers (click to zoom in/out)

Clutch Cable

The clutch cable makes a secure connection to the clutch pedal. Strong steel wire is used. Movement of the pedal is, therefore, transferred to the release bearing. A few vehicles use hydraulics to operate the clutch.

A cable connects the pedal to the bearing (click to zoom in/out)

Cable Seating Plate and Pad

A support is made for the ball end of the cable. Many different methods are used, and this is just one example. A rubber pad prevents metal-to-metal contact. A retaining clip secures the end of the cable.

Many methods are used (click to zoom in/out)

Bell Housing

A general cover is used for the clutch assembly, but it is also the way to secure the clutch and gearbox to the engine. Some front-wheel drive clutches are covered with a thin, pressed steel plate.

Cover for the clutch assembly (click to zoom in/out)

Summary

The clutch is a device for disconnecting and connecting drive from the engine. It allows a temporary neutral position for gear changes and a gradual way of taking up drive from rest.

Clutch components

Read the last few pages again and note down FIVE bullet points here:

KC   State the purpose of a release bearing.

Section 3. Clutch Operating Mechanisms

Introduction

The driver operates the clutch by pushing down a pedal. This movement has to be transferred to the release mechanism. There are two main methods used. These are cable and hydraulic. The cable method is the most common. Now under development, electrically operated clutches will soon be readily available.

Clutch pedal operation

Cable

A steel cable is used, which runs inside a plastic-coated steel tube. The cable "outer" must be fixed at each end. The cable "inner" transfers the movement. One problem with cable clutches is that movement of the engine with respect to the vehicle body can cause the length to change. This results in a judder/vibration when the clutch is used. This problem has been almost eliminated by careful positioning and by quality engine mountings.

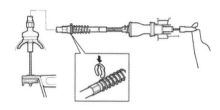

Clutch cable[1]

Cable Operation

This clutch cable works on a simple lever principle. The clutch pedal is the first lever. Movement is transferred from the pedal to the second lever, which is the release fork. The fork, in turn, moves the release bearing to operate the clutch.

Cable movement

Hydraulic

A hydraulic mechanism involves two cylinders. These are termed the master and slave cylinders. The master cylinder is connected to the clutch pedal. The slave cylinder is connected to the release lever.

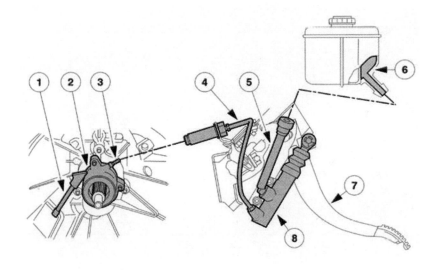

Clutch hydraulic components[1]

Hydraulic Operation

The clutch pedal moves the master cylinder piston. This pushes fluid through a pipe, which in turn forces a piston out of the slave cylinder. The movement ratio can be set by the cylinder diameters and the lever ratios.

Hydraulic movement

Read the last few pages again and note down FIVE bullet points here:

Electronic Clutch

The electronic clutch was developed for racing vehicles to improve the getaway performance. For production vehicles, a strategy has been developed to interpret the driver's intention. With greater throttle openings, the strategy changes to prevent abuse and drive line damage. Electrical control of the clutch-release bearing position is by a solenoid actuator, which can be modulated by signals from the ECU. This reduces the time needed to reach the ideal take-off position and the ability of the clutch to transmit torque is improved. Efficiency of the whole system can therefore be increased.

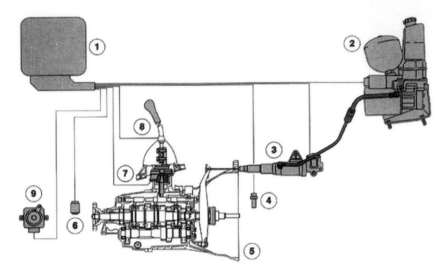

Electronically operated clutch[1]

KC   Describe the operation of a hydraulic clutch mechanism.

Module 2. Clutch Components
Section 1. Diaphragm Clutch

Basic Functions

A clutch is a device for disconnecting and connecting rotating shafts. In a vehicle with a manual gearbox, the driver pushes down the clutch when changing gears to disconnect the engine from the gearbox. It also allows a temporary neutral position for, say, waiting at traffic lights and a gradual way of taking up drive from rest.

Diaphragm clutch

Clutch Location

The exact location of the clutch varies with vehicle design. However, the clutch is always fitted between the engine and the transmission. With few exceptions, the clutch and flywheel are bolted to the rear of the engine crankshaft.

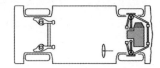

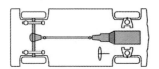

Typical positions for the clutch

Main Parts

The clutch is made of two main parts: a pressure plate and a driven plate. The driven plate, often called the clutch disc, is fitted on the shaft, which takes the drive into the gearbox.

Driven plate and pressure plate

Engagement

When the clutch is engaged, the pressure plate presses the driven plate against the engine flywheel. This allows drive to be passed to the gearbox. Depressing the clutch moves the pressure plate away, which frees the driven plate.

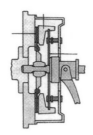 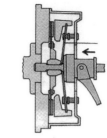

Clutch engaged   Clutch disengaged

Coil Springs

Earlier clutches (and some heavy-duty types) use coil springs instead of a diaphragm. However, the diaphragm clutch replaced the coil-spring type because it has the following advantages:

It is not affected by high speeds. (Coil springs can be thrown outward.)

The low pedal force makes for easy operation.

It is light and compact.

The clamping force increases or at least remains constant as the friction lining on the plate wears.

Coil spring clutch assembly

Movement of the Diaphragm Clutch

The animation shows the movement of the diaphragm during clutch operation. The method of controlling the clutch is quite simple. The mechanism consists of either a cable or a hydraulic system.

Clutch operation

Clutch Shaft

The clutch shaft, or gearbox input shaft, extends from the front of the gearbox. Most shafts have a smaller section or spigot, which extends from its outer end. This rides in a spigot bearing in the engine crankshaft flange. The splined area of the shaft allows the clutch disc to move along the splines. When the clutch is engaged, the disc drives the gearbox input shaft through these splines.

Gearbox input shaft

Clutch Disc

The clutch disc is a steel plate covered with frictional material. It fits between the flywheel face and the pressure plate. In the center of the disc is the hub, which is splined to fit over the splines of the input shaft. As the clutch is engaged, the disc is firmly squeezed between the flywheel and pressure plate. Power from the engine is transmitted by the hub to the gearbox input shaft. The width of the hub prevents the disc from rocking on the shaft as it moves along the shaft.

Clutch disc or driven plate

Frictional Facings

The clutch disc has frictional material riveted or bonded on both sides. These frictional facings are either woven or molded. Molded facings are preferred because they can withstand high-pressure plate-loading forces. Grooves are cut across the face of the friction facings to allow for smooth clutch action and increased cooling. The cuts also make a place for the facing dust to go as the clutch lining material wears.

Friction material

Health Hazards

The frictional material wears as the clutch is engaged. At one time asbestos was commonly used. Because of the health hazards resulting from asbestos, new lining materials have been developed. The most commonly used types are paper-based and ceramic materials. They are strengthened by the addition of cotton and brass particles and wire. These additives increase the torsional strength of the facings and prolong the life of the clutch.

Danger – asbestos!

Wave Springs

The facings are attached to wave springs, which cause the contact pressure on the facings to rise gradually. This is because the springs flatten out when the clutch is engaged. These springs eliminate chatter when the clutch is engaged. They also help to move the disc away from the flywheel when it is disengaged. The wave springs and facings are attached to the steel disc.

These springs eliminate chatter

Types of Clutch Discs

There are two types of clutch discs: rigid and flexible. A rigid clutch disc is a solid circular disc fastened directly to a center splined hub. The flexible clutch disc has torsional dampener springs that circle the center hub. s

Solid and flexible discs

Shock Absorbing

The dampener is a shock-absorbing feature built into a flexible clutch disc. The primary purpose of the flexible disc is to absorb power impulses from the engine that would otherwise be transmitted directly to the gears in the transmission. A flexible clutch disc has torsion springs and friction discs between the plate and hub of the clutch.

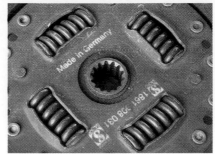
Damping springs

Sudden Loading

When the clutch is engaged, the springs cushion the sudden loading by flexing and allowing some twist between the hub and plate. When the loading is over, the springs release and the disc transmits power normally. The number, and tension, of these springs is determined by the amount of engine torque and the weight of the vehicle. Stop pins limit this torsional movement to a few millimeters.

The springs cushion a sudden loading

Pressure Plate Assembly

The pressure plate squeezes the clutch disc onto the flywheel when the clutch is engaged. It moves away from the disc when the clutch is disengaged. These actions allow the clutch disc to transmit, or not transmit, the engine's torque to the gearbox.

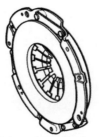
Details of the pressure plate

Spring Loading

A pressure plate is a large spring-loaded clamp that is bolted to, and rotates with, the flywheel. The assembly includes a metal cover, heavy release springs, and a metal pressure ring that provides a friction surface for the clutch disc. It also includes a thrust ring or fingers for the release bearing, and release levers.

Pressure plate

Release Levers

The release levers release the holding force of the springs when the clutch is disengaged. Some pressure plates are of a "semi-centrifugal" design. They use centrifugal weights, which increase the clamping force on the thrust springs as engine speed increases.

Levers release the holding force

Diaphragm Spring

The diaphragm spring assembly is a cone-shaped diaphragm spring between the pressure plate and the cover. Its purpose is to clamp the pressure plate against the clutch disc. This spring is normally secured to the cover by rivets. When pressure is exerted on the center of the spring, the outer diameter of the spring tends to straighten out. When pressure is released, the spring resumes its normal cone shape.

Cone-shaped diaphragm spring

Clutch Release

The center portion of the spring is slit into a number of fingers that act as release levers. When the clutch is disengaged, these fingers are depressed by the release bearing. The diaphragm spring pivots over a fulcrum ring. This makes its outer rim move away from the flywheel. The retracting springs pull the pressure plate away from the clutch disc to disengage the clutch.

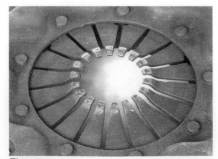

Fingers

Clutch Engagement

As the clutch is engaged, the release bearing is moved away from the release fingers. As the spring pivots over the fulcrum ring, its outer rim forces the pressure plate tightly against the clutch disc. At this point, the clutch disc is clamped between the flywheel and pressure plate.

Release bearing movement

Read the last few pages again and note down FIVE bullet points here:

Clutch Assembly

The individual parts of a pressure plate assembly are contained in the cover. Most covers are vented to allow heat to escape and air to enter. Other covers are designed to provide a fan action to force air circulation around the clutch assembly. The effectiveness of the clutch is affected by heat. Therefore, by allowing the assembly to cool, it works better.

Clutch cover

KC   Describe the shock absorbing features of a clutch disc.

Coil Spring Pressure Plate

Coil spring pressure plate assemblies use helical springs that are evenly spaced around the inside of the pressure plate cover. These springs exert pressure to hold the pressure plate against the flywheel.

Coil spring clutch

Release Levers

During clutch disengagement, levers release the holding force of the springs and the clutch disc no longer rotates with the pressure plate and flywheel. Usually, these pressure plates have three release levers. Each lever has two pivot points.

Disengagement levers

Pivot Point

One pivot point attaches the lever to a pedestal cast into the pressure plate. The other attaches the lever to a release yoke that is bolted to the cover. The levers pivot on the pedestals and release lever yokes. This moves the pressure plate through its engagement and disengagement operations.

Each lever has two pivot points

Disengagement

To disengage the clutch, the release bearing pushes the inner ends of the release levers toward the flywheel. The outer ends of the release levers move to pull the pressure plate away from the clutch disc. This action compresses the coil springs and disengages the clutch.

The bearing pushes the release levers

Engagement

When the clutch is engaged, the release bearing moves and allows the springs to exert pressure. This holds the pressure plate against the clutch disc, which in turn forces the disc against the flywheel. The engine power is therefore transmitted to the gearbox through the clutch disc.

The disc is forced against the flywheel

Read the last few pages again and note down FIVE bullet points here:

KC   Describe how a clutch is disengaged.

Introduction

The simple definition of a clutch is something that engages or disengages drive. A number of different types of clutches are used for this purpose. Some of these are examined briefly on the following screens.

Clutch in use

Notes

Automatic Transmission

Automatic transmissions use a torque converter, or fluid flywheel, to couple the engine and the gearbox. The torque converter is a fluid coupling in which one rotating part causes transmission fluid to rotate. This imparts a rotation to another part, which is connected to the gearbox.

Automatic gearbox

Torque Converter

The coupling action of the torque converter, or fluid clutch, allows slippage for when the car is starting from rest. As the car gains speed, the slippage is reduced, and at cruising speeds, the driven member turns almost as fast as the driving member does. Some modern systems lock the two together at high speed to eliminate slip. An automatic gearbox usually contains epicyclic or planetary gears. Clutches and brake bands are used for engaging the desired gears.

Fluid clutch

Multiplate Clutches

Multiplate clutches are used in specialized applications such as for very high-performance vehicles. Some motorcycles and heavy commercial vehicles also use clutches of this type. The principle is the same as a single-plate clutch, except that with multiple plates, greater power can be transmitted.

Motor-cycle clutch

Automatic Gearbox Clutch

A common use of a multiplate clutch is in an automatic gearbox. This is because a number of clutches are needed to control the gears. As space is limited, multiple plates are used to allow all of the power to be transmitted. Modern limited-slip differentials also make use of the multiplate clutch technique.

Clutches as part of an automatic gearbox[2]

High-Performance Clutch

Many high-performance clutch assemblies use multiple-clutch discs. An intermediate plate is used in these assemblies to separate the clutch discs.

A good clutch is important[2]

Operation

When the clutch is engaged, the first clutch disc is held between the clutch pressure plate and intermediate plate, and the second clutch disc is held between the intermediate plate and the flywheel. When disengaged, the intermediate plate, flywheel, and pressure plate assembly rotate as a unit, while the clutch discs, which are not in contact with the plates, rotate freely within the assembly and do not transmit power to the transmission.

High-performance clutch (Delphi)

Summary

A clutch will continue to work for many miles of trouble-free driving. However, a sensible driving technique and regular quick checks can help to avoid problems.

Not the recommended driving technique!

Read the last few pages again and note down FIVE bullet points here:

KC   Describe the operation of a multiplate clutch as it is engaged.

Safety First

Before carrying out any service or repair work, refer to all appropriate health and safety guidelines. Always follow all safety procedures and observe safety precautions when working on vehicles. Some of the specific hazards associated with clutch work are listed in this section. General safety advice is also included.

Jacking the car

Notes

Asbestos

Like many types of brake-lining material, some friction discs contain asbestos fibers. Always follow safety precautions when handling asbestos.

Breathing mask in use

Running Engines

Running engines are sometimes needed for diagnostics and system checks. A running engine presents two hazards: The first is the risk from rotating components and the second from the accumulation of exhaust gas in the workshop. Remain aware of rotating parts such as the fan, belt, and pulleys in the areas where you are likely to be working.

Be aware of moving parts

Electrically Driven Fans

An electrically driven fan is switched on automatically when the temperature of the coolant in the radiator rises above the switch operating temperature. This can occur even when the ignition is switched off. Always keep fingers out of the fan cowl and, for diagnostic tests, always remove the battery ground cable when the engine does not need to be running.

Fans can start at any time

Exhaust Emissions

When running an engine, it is important to prevent the build-up of exhaust gas in the workshop. Use extraction equipment that has special adapters for the gas probe or provide good ventilation.

Extraction equipment

Hot Components

When used for prolonged periods, vehicle components can become very hot. In particular, be careful not to touch the exhaust when working on clutch systems.

Be aware of hot exhausts

Working Under Vehicles

There are a number of hazards to avoid when working under vehicles. One is the very high temperature of exhaust, which can cause severe burns. Another risk is the possibility of getting rust and dirt in the eyes. Avoid these problems by keeping clear of hot surfaces and by wearing goggles. The vehicle must be supported safely before working underneath or alongside it.

Car on a ramp

Heavy Loads

Any job that requires the lifting and moving of heavy loads carries with it a certain amount of risk. Many gearboxes fall into this category. Always tackle these jobs in an appropriate manner by making sure you use the recommended lifting equipment. Ask for assistance if necessary.

Gearbox

Jacking and Supporting

Only use the recommended jacking and support points when lifting a vehicle. Refer to the manufacturer's instructions if unsure. Ensure that the jack and support stands, which must be used at all times, have an appropriate safe working load (SWL).

Jack and support point

Skin Contact

When servicing vehicle systems, avoid skin contact with new and used engine oils. Use barrier cream or non-porous gloves. Be careful with hot oil, particularly when carrying out oil-draining operations. Never keep oily rags in overalls or other pockets and change out of oil-contaminated clothing as soon as reasonably possible. Dust from brakes can be dangerous; wear a breathing mask if necessary.

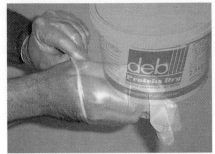
Wear gloves or use barrier cream

Caution-Attention-Achtung!

All types of fuel – and particularly the vapors – are highly flammable. They can be ignited from a number of sources. Any exposed flame, a cigarette, and, under the right conditions, even a hot object will start a fire.

Take care!

Electrical Sparks

The most common cause of vehicle fires in the workshop is from electrical sparks. These can occur during the connection and removal of electrical terminals. Sparks also occur when the engine is cranked with the ignition on and the spark plugs removed. Disconnect the coil or connect the HT cables directly to ground to prevent this.

Sparks from the battery lead

Original Equipment

In consideration of other people's property, always be careful to use approved parts. Original equipment manufacturer's (OEM) parts may be required to meet safety regulations.

Use good quality parts

Read the last few pages again and note down FIVE bullet points here:

Scheduled Servicing

Scheduled service requirements for the clutch are quite simple. The clutch should be checked for correct operation and the adjustment set if required. The clutch pedal should be secure and operate correctly.

Clutch components need routine maintenance

Non-Routine Work

When carrying out routine maintenance, some non-routine work may be necessary. This should be reported to the driver or owner of the vehicle before repairs are carried out.

Seriously damaged clutch!

Workshop Tasks

Worksheets for routine maintenance of the clutch are included in this program. Refer to the safety precautions in the Health and Safety sections before carrying out any practical work on vehicles. The worksheets can be printed and used as part of a practical training program. They give general instructions. Therefore, they only should be used along with a manufacturer's workshop manual or other good source of information.

Refer to other sources of data as necessary

Worksheet

Check and adjust clutch freeplay.

The freeplay on a clutch is to ensure that it will always fully engage. Initial symptoms of a problem include a slipping clutch, if not enough freeplay, or difficult gear changing, if too much. Check manufacturer's data for the correct setting.

Clutch lever movement

Pedal Height

Pedal height is usually altered by adjusting a stop bolt. This is located on the pedal box in the driver's foot well. Check manufacturer's data for the correct setting.

Pedal box

Cable Components

The cable and automatic adjustment mechanism should be visually inspected for signs of wear or damage. A cable that is fraying should be replaced. Some automatic adjusters have teeth, which can wear out after prolonged use.

Clutch cable

Hydraulic Components

Visually inspect all hydraulic components. Look for signs of fluid leaking from the master cylinder, pipes, and slave cylinder. Repair any faults found. Top off the reservoir if need be.

Slave cylinder

Clutch Adjustment

Checking clutch freeplay is easier with an assistant. Check carefully how far the pedal moves before the clutch lever moves. Adjust to recommended settings where possible.

Checking the clutch lever

Automatic Adjuster

Automatic adjusters do not often need attention. However, repair or replace the automatic adjuster if freeplay is incorrect. There are two main types: One uses a ratchet pawl and the other works with a sleeve on the cable.

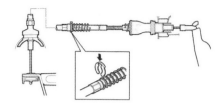

Cable adjuster[1]

Bleeding the Hydraulics

Hydraulic systems may need some extra work. If the feel of the clutch pedal becomes "spongy" it may be necessary to bleed air out of the system. This is done by connecting a rubber tube to a bleed nipple on the slave cylinder. The other end of the tube is placed in a container holding a small amount of fluid. The clutch pedal is pumped slowly until all the air is expelled. Remember to keep the reservoir topped off during this process.

Pipe connected to the slave cylinder

Read the last few pages again and note down FIVE bullet points here:

Topping Off

Always use the fluid recommended by the manufacturer. Be particularly careful not to spill fluid, which will damage paintwork. The same type of hydraulic fluid is usually used for the clutch and the brake systems.

Hydraulic fluid

Clutch reservoir

Summary

Safety of all road users and pedestrians is essential. Reliable operation of the vehicle is also important. Therefore, the condition of the clutch is vital. Carry out a check at all service intervals.

Safety is important[2]

Regular Checks

Regular checks are vital for a customer's safety. Carry these out at all service checks and report your findings to the customer. Advise customers if the clutch will need attention before the next scheduled service interval.

Explain to the customer any unusual conditions

Driving Style

Driving style can have a significant effect on the life and condition of a clutch. Customers, of course, are entitled to drive how they wish! However, it may be appropriate to offer tactful advice if a clutch, or driveline component, breaks unexpectedly. Rapid starts, for example, can cause damage to a number of components.

Style not recommended!

Slipping the Clutch

Holding a car with the clutch slipping (on a hill at traffic lights, for example) increases the wear rate. Again, it may be appropriate to offer tactful advice if a clutch wears out before its expected life. Make sure you don't insult the driver.

Stop and apply the parking brake!

Clutch Feel

Tell your customers to report any changes in the "feel" of the clutch pedal. Have them contact a service center if, for example, the clutch becomes stiff or a noise is noticed. These may be early warning signs of problems. Reporting them could help the driver avoid the inconvenience of a breakdown.

Pedal movement

Vehicle Condition

Respect your customers' vehicles and take precautions to keep them clean. Checking and repairing the clutch is likely to involve you working under the vehicle, and then sitting in the driver's seat. Use seat covers and ensure the steering wheel is cleaned when you have finished.

Seat covers in use

Read the last few pages again and note down FIVE bullet points here:

Summary

A customer who is kept informed and treated with respect will return and keep you in a job! Explain things to a customer when asked – it will be appreciated.

A happy customer will return

Notes

Introduction

System performance checks are routine activities that occur during all servicing work. They start at pre-delivery and continue for all scheduled service intervals.

Clutch systems may need checking[2]

Quick Checks

Quick checks must be thorough, as they are looking for incorrect operation or adjustment and the first signs of deterioration. Detailed diagnostic procedures may be required to identify faulty components. Always refer to manufacturer's data when necessary.

Manufacturer's data

Workshop Tasks

Worksheets for checking the performance of the clutch are included in this program. Refer to the safety precautions in the Health and Safety sections before carrying out any practical work on vehicles. The worksheets can be printed and used as part of a practical training program. They give general instructions only. Therefore, they should be used together with a manufacturer's workshop manual or some other good source of information.

Refer to other sources of data as necessary

Worksheet

Check clutch for chatter/judder.

Apply the parking brake, depress the clutch and start the engine. Select first gear and increase the engine speed to about 1,500 rev/min. Slowly release the clutch pedal and note clutch operation as the pressure plate first makes contact. Select reverse gear and repeat the test. If chatter/judder occurs, raise the vehicle on a hoist for further inspection.

Checking for clutch judder

Judder or Chatter

Check for loose engine mountings, loose or missing bellhousing bolts and for a damaged linkage. Correct any faults found. Lower the vehicle and repeat the test procedure. If no faults are found then the clutch may have to be removed and replaced.

Checking engine mountings

Worksheet

Check for clutch drag.

Apply parking brake, depress the clutch, and start the engine. Select first gear but do not release the clutch. Next, select neutral but again do not release the clutch. Wait ten seconds, select reverse and check for a clash.

Clutch depressed

Drag

If a clash is noticed, check the clutch linkage. Correct any faults found with the linkage and repeat the previous tests. If no faults are found then the clutch may have to be removed and components replaced.

Checking the clutch linkage

Worksheet

Check clutch for slippage.

Apply the parking brake and chock all wheels. Run the engine until it reaches normal operating temperature. Select a high gear (e.g., fourth) and run the engine at about 2,000 rev/min. Release the clutch pedal slowly until, if possible, it is fully engaged.

Read the last few pages again and note down FIVE bullet points here:

Chock the wheels securely

Slippage

The engine should stall when the previous test is carried out. If not, raise vehicle on a lift and check clutch linkage. Correct any problems found. If the linkage was at fault, repeat the previous tests. If the linkage is in order, then the clutch will have to be removed for repair.

Testing for clutch slippage

Worksheet

Check for clutch pedal pulsation.

Apply the parking brake and start the engine. Slowly depress the clutch until it just begins to disengage. Note any pedal pulsations (some minor pulsations are to be expected). Depress further and, again, note any pedal pulsations.

Pedal pulsation

Pulsation

If pulsations are noted during the test, check the crankshaft damper and other engine ancillaries. Correct any faults and repeat the above tests. If all is in order, then the clutch will have to be removed for repair.

Crankshaft damper pulley

Ancillaries drive belts

Summary

System checks for the clutch are quite simple. However, they are important. Cars are operated at relatively high speed on freeways and breakdowns can be dangerous. Therefore, it is important that the systems function correctly at all times.

Busy traffic!

Introduction

Some special test equipment is used when working with clutches. Remember, you should always refer to the manufacturer's instructions appropriate to the equipment you are using.

Refer to manufacturer's instructions

Dial Test Gauge

A dial test gauge or dial test indicator (DTI) is a useful piece of measuring equipment. It is usually used in conjunction with a magnetic stand. As the needle is moved, the dial (via a series of accurate gears) indicates the distance traveled. The graduations are either hundredths of a millimeter or thousandths of an inch.

DTI[5]   Stand[5]

Straight Edge and Feelers

A "straight edge" is, quite simply, a piece of equipment with a straight edge! It is used as a reference for measuring flatness. The straight edge is placed on top of the test subject. The feeler blades are then used to assess the size of any gaps. The feeler blades are sized in either hundredths of a millimeter or thousandths of an inch.

Straight edge[5]

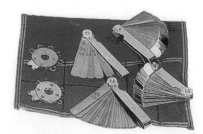

Feeler set[5]

Micrometer and Vernier Caliper

A metric micrometer is a measuring instrument designed to measure to an accuracy of 0.01 mm. Its principle of operation is quite simple: A very accurately manufactured screw thread is used with a pitch of 0.5 mm. This means that as it is rotated, one complete turn will move it 0.5 mm. A main scale is marked on the micrometer with 0.5 mm marks. A rotating scale marked from 0 to 50 is used to give the required accuracy. The Vernier caliper works on the principle of two offset scales. It is also capable of giving accurate readings.

Caliper and micrometer kit[5]

Read the last few pages again and note down FIVE bullet points here:

Caliper and Dividers

Caliper and dividers are simple non-indication measuring tools. They are normally used to compare one size to another. They may be useful for checking a pilot/spigot bearing size, for example.

Machinist's caliper[5]   Dividers[5]

Accuracy

To ensure that measuring equipment remains accurate, there are just two simple guidelines:

Handle the equipment with care. A micrometer thrown on the floor will not be accurate.

Ensure that instruments are calibrated regularly. This means checking them regularly against equipment known to be in good working order.

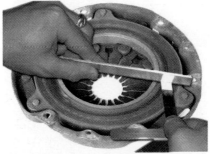

Straight edge and feelers in use

Introduction

The secret to finding faults is to have a good knowledge of the system and to work in a logical way. Use manufacturer's data and recommended procedures. This section includes general faultfinding procedures, and specific ones for clutches.

Check data before starting work

Symptoms and Faults

Remember a symptom is the observed result of a fault. The following four screens each state a common symptom and possible faults.

Symptoms are the result of faults

Clutch Slipping

Possible causes of this symptom are:

Clutch worn out

Clutch adjustment is incorrect

Oil contamination on the linings

Consider these and other possibilities when carrying out faultfinding work on a slipping clutch.

Worn clutch disc

Difficult to Change Gears

Possible causes of this symptom are:

Clutch out of adjustment

Clutch hydraulic fault, such as a leak

Gearbox selectors worn

Consider these and other possibilities when carrying out faultfinding work on a clutch, which may not be disengaging correctly.

Slave cylinder

Clutch Drag

Possible causes of this symptom are:

Clutch out of adjustment

Pressure plate springs and/or fingers are worn

Consider these and other possibilities when carrying out faultfinding work on a clutch, which may be dragging.

Worn clutch fingers

Systematic Testing

Working through a logical and planned systematic procedure for testing a system is the only reliable way to diagnose a problem. Use these six stages of faultfinding as a guide.

Verify the fault

Collect further information

Evaluate the evidence

Carry out further tests in a logical sequence

Fix the problem

Check all systems

Stages of faultfinding

Faultfinding Procedure

As an example of how the stages are applied, assume the reported symptom is that the clutch is slipping. The recommended method would be to carry out the procedures outlined on the next five screens.

Check the latest data

Verify the Fault

Road test to confirm when the symptoms occur. Alternatively, test the vehicle in the workshop. This procedure is described in the Checking System Performance section. It is important to develop a good idea of exactly what the problem is.

Road test in progress

Collect Further Information

Look for oil leaking from the bell housing or general area of the clutch. However, external oil leaks would not necessarily affect the clutch. Check the clutch for correct adjustment. If an automatic adjuster is fitted, make sure this is operating correctly.

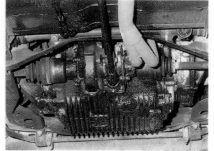

This oil leak is cause for concern!

Evaluate the Evidence

At this stage, stop and consider what you know. For example, if no oil leaks are apparent, and if adjustment is correct, the clutch must be examined. If this is the case, the transmission will have to be removed.

Transmission components

Carry out Further Tests

Once the clutch is exposed, further tests can be carried out. If the adjustment was incorrect or oil was noted, check these aspects in more detail. However, following the given example, the clutch assembly must now be removed. A simple visual examination may be all that is required.

Flywheel   Clutch disc   Pressure plate   Release bearing

Rectify the Problem

At this stage, parts should be replaced or repaired as necessary. If replacement is required, this is often done with a kit that consists of the clutch plate, a cover, and a bearing. The transmission system can now be rebuilt.

Clutch repair kit

Check All Systems

It is very important, when work has been completed, to check that all systems are operating correctly. It is also important to check that no other problems have been created! Road test and check the operation of the clutch and complete transmission system to make sure everything is in good working order.

Road test

Summary

Faultfinding work is rewarding – when you find the fault! Remember to always work in a logical way. The stages of faultfinding can be applied to all systems, and that includes the clutch.

Clutch in position

Read the last few pages again and note down FIVE bullet points here:

Module 5. Component Inspection and Repair
Section 1. Tools and Equipment

Introduction

The abbreviation R&R is short for remove and refit components, or remove and reassemble components. Components will usually be removed, inspected, and repaired or replaced when a defect has been diagnosed. Other components are replaced, or stripped and cleaned, at scheduled mileage or time intervals. Refer to the Routine Maintenance section for details on these items.

Good tools and equipment are important[2]

Procedures

The descriptions provided in this section deal with the components for individual replacement, rather than as a part of other work. Always refer to a workshop manual before starting work. You will also need to look for the recommended procedure, special tools, materials, tightening sequences, and torque settings. Some of the common tools and pieces of equipment are described on the following screens.

Refer to data as required

Torque Wrench

A good torque wrench is an essential piece of equipment. Many types are available but all work on a similar principle. Most are set by adjusting a screwed cylinder, which forms part of the handle. An important point to remember is that, as with any measuring tool, regular calibration is essential to ensure that it remains accurate.

A torque wrench is a useful tool[5]

Air Guns

The whole point of power tools is that they do the work so you don't have to! Most air guns have an aluminum housing. This material is lightweight but will last a long time. Air guns produce a "hammer" action. Because of this, impact sockets should be used. Normal sockets can shatter under this load. It is important to remember that air tools need lubricating from time to time.

Wheel gun in use

Jacks and Stands

Most jacks are simple hydraulic devices. Remember to make sure the safe working load (SWL) is not exceeded. Ensure that any faults with equipment such as this are reported immediately. Axle stands must always be placed under the vehicle supporting the weight before work is carried out.

Always use stands...[5]

After jacking a vehicle[5]

Ramps and Hoists

Many ramps are available ranging from large four-post wheel-free types to smaller single-post lifts. These large items should be inspected regularly to ensure that they are safe.

Twin-post lift[5]

Transmission Jack

If a complete gearbox has to be removed, it is likely to be heavy! A transmission jack has attachments that allow you to support the gearbox and lower it safely. The equipment is hydraulically operated just like an ordinary jack. Often, the height can be set by using a foot pedal, which leaves both hands free for positioning the unit.

This jack will support a gearbox[5]

Clutch Aligner Kit

The clutch disc must be aligned with the cover and flywheel when it is fitted. If not, it is almost impossible on some vehicles to replace the gearbox. This is because the gearbox shaft has to fit through the disc and into the pilot or spigot bearing in the flywheel. The kit shown here has adaptors to suit most vehicles.

The clutch must be aligned when fitted

Pilot/Spigot Bearing Puller

Removing spigot bearings is difficult without a proper puller. This tool has small legs and feet that hook under the bearing. A threaded section is tightened to pull out the bearing.

An internal bearing puller[5]

Air Ratchet

These tools are very useful for removing or fitting nuts and bolts. However, it is possible to overtighten if care is not taken. Air tools can be very powerful and will trap your hands! Take adequate precautions at all times.

These tools are very useful[5]

Read the last few pages again and note down FIVE bullet points here:

Introduction

The main inspections and measurements carried on the system are included in this section. Inspections should take place at scheduled service intervals, and anytime problems have been reported.

 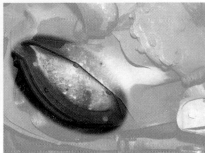

Clutch positions...   Vary...

Workshop Tasks

Worksheets for inspections and measurement of the system are included in this section. Refer to the safety precautions in the Health and Safety sections before carrying out any practical work on vehicles. The worksheets can be printed and used as part of a practical training program. They give general instructions only and should therefore be used together with a manufacturer's workshop manual, or some other good source of information.

Refer to other sources of data as necessary

Worksheet

Replace clutch assembly.

Always obtain and follow the manufacturer's procedures for work such as this. The first job is to disconnect the battery (earth first) and fit a memory keeper if necessary. The procedure outlined here is generic and therefore may not be applicable to all vehicles.

Clutch and gearbox in position

Supporting the Vehicle

The vehicle must be supported on a hoist for most clutch removal jobs. Ensure that it is securely positioned and that the wheels are chocked. Remove the starter motor and driveline components.

Car on a hoist

Transmission Removal

Remove the clutch cable or the slave cylinder if used. Remove the transmission components, following procedures at all times. It may be necessary, on some vehicles, to support the engine. This is because some gearbox mountings also support the engine. Remove the clutch fork and release bearing assembly.

Remove the clutch cable

Clutch Cover and Plate

Remove any dust using recommended health procedures. Mark the clutch cover if necessary and remove the ring of bolts. Remove the clutch cover and plate. Inspect, repair, or replace as necessary. It is usual to replace the plate, cover, and bearing as a set, but not essential.

Removing the clutch cover

Flywheel Condition

Check the condition of the flywheel using a dial gauge. It is possible for the flywheel to become warped due to excessive heat from a slipping clutch. Refer to manufacturers' data for the maximum permissible runout.

Check the flywheel contact surface

Alignment

Select the correct alignment tool for the spigot bearing and disc. The small end of the tool fits into the spigot bearing and the larger diameter fits inside the splines of the disc. Using the alignment tool, replace the disc and cover. Secure the cover with the ring of bolts, setting them to the correct torque.

  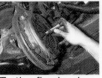 

Align and...   Fit the clutch...   To the flywheel...   And secure the bolts

Testing

Refit all the transmission components in a reverse of the removal process. Set the clutch freeplay to the manufacturer's recommended value. Test the clutch operation in the workshop and then on a road test.

Job finished!

Read the last few pages again and note down FIVE bullet points here:

•

Section 3. Inspect and Measure Components

Introduction

The main inspections and measurements carried out on the system are included in this section. Inspections should take place at scheduled service intervals, and anytime problems have been reported.

Inspections and measurements are important[2a]

Workshop Tasks

Worksheets for inspections and measurement of the system are included in this section. Refer to the safety precautions in the Health and Safety sections before carrying out any practical work on vehicles. The worksheets can be printed and used as part of a practical training program. They give general instructions only and should therefore be used together with a manufacturer's workshop manual, or some other good source of information.

Refer to data as required

Clutch Adjustment

Checking clutch freeplay is easier with an assistant. Look at how far the pedal moves before the clutch lever moves. Adjust to recommended settings where possible. Most systems, however, have an automatic adjuster mechanism. Ensure that this is operating correctly.

Checking the clutch lever

Fluid Condition

Brake and clutch fluid is hygroscopic. This means that it absorbs water. For this reason, the fluid may need to be changed periodically. Follow manufacturer's recommendations.

Brake/Clutch fluid

Worksheet

Inspect and measure clutch components.

It is important to visually check all parts for scoring, burning, and other faults before carrying out measurements. If in any doubt, it's a good idea to replace the components.

Clutch cover and pressure plate

Cover Warping

Check the flywheel cover for warping by using a straightedge and a set of feelers. Place a straightedge across the pressure plate and check any gaps using the feelers. Compare to specifications and, if excessive, replace the cover.

Straight edge and feelers in use

Flywheel Run-Out

Check the flywheel for run-out by fitting a dial test gauge to the rear of the engine. Use a magnetic stand to ensure that the gauge is held still. Set the gauge against the flywheel and rotate one full revolution by hand. Note the readings and compare to manufacturer's specifications. It is possible to skim a flywheel if necessary.

Flywheel   DTI[5]

Spigot Bearing Freeplay

The freeplay in the spigot or pilot bearing can be tested by using the correct alignment adaptor. Rock the tool left to right and gauge the movement. Some movement is to be expected; however, if in any doubt, replace the bearing.

Spigot bearings

Alignment kit

Lining Thickness

In most cases, the thickness of the clutch plate friction material can be assessed by eye. However, it may be necessary to make a measurement using a caliper gauge. Compare this to manufacturer's data.

Clutch plate

Lining Condition

Linings can become contaminated with oil. The usual cause of this problem is a leak from the rear main crankshaft oil seal. This should be replaced if it is showing any signs of leakage.

Crankshaft oil seal

Summary

Clutch repairs can involve significant work. However, do not make any compromises. Keep your customers – and yourself – happy and safe.

Job finished!

Read the last few pages again and note down FIVE bullet points here:

TOPIC: MANUAL GEARBOX

Module 1. Manual Transmission Principles
Section 1. Introduction to Transmission

Introduction

Transmission is a general term used to describe all of the components required to transmit power from the engine to the wheels. The requirement is to convert the power from the relatively high velocity and low torque of the engine crankshaft to the variable, usually lower speed and higher torque needed at the wheels. This first section is a general introduction to the transmission system.

Notes

Transmission components are important[2]

Types of Transmission

The two basic types of transmissions use either a manual gearbox, in which the gears are selected by the driver, or an automatic gearbox, in which the gears are changed automatically. The other driveline components, with the exception of the clutch, are the same for automatic and manual systems.

Manual transmission   Automatic transmission

Front-Wheel Drive Transmission

Working from the engine to the wheels, the main components of a typical front-wheel drive transmission system are:

Clutch

Gearbox

Final drive and differential

Driveshafts.

Clutch   Gearbox   Final drive and differential   Driveshaft

Rear-Wheel Drive Transmission

Working from the engine to the wheels, the main components of a typical rear-wheel drive transmission system are:

Clutch

Gearbox

Propshaft

Final drive and differential

Half shafts

Clutch   Gearbox²   Propshaft   Final drive and differential

Clutch

The clutch is fitted between the engine and gearbox. It allows the drive to be disconnected when the pedal is depressed. This is often described as a temporary neutral. The clutch also allows a smooth take-up of drive and gears to be changed.

Clutch assembly

Manual Gearbox

A manual gearbox is a box full of gears of varying ratios. The gear ratio most suitable for the driving conditions is selected by the driver. Most boxes contain about 13 gear cogs, which allow five forward gears and one reverse.

Click to zoom in on the gearbox components

Torque Converter

A torque converter is sometimes called a fluid flywheel (although the two differ slightly) and is used in conjunction with an automatic gearbox. It is in two main parts. As the input section rotates, fluid pressure begins to act on the output section, which is made to rotate. As speed increases, a better drive is made. The drive therefore takes up automatically and smoothly.

Details of a torque converter

Automatic Gearbox

As the name suggests, this is a gearbox that operates automatically. Most types contain special gear arrangements, known as epicyclic gear trains. Some now use complicated electronic control, but the basic principle is that fluid pressure from a pump, which changes with road speed, is used to change the gears.

Epicyclic gears are often used in an 'auto-box'

Final Drive

To produce the required torque at the road wheels, a fixed gear reduction from the high engine speed is required. The final drive consists of just two gears with a ratio of about 4:1. These are bevel gears on rear-wheel drive systems and normal gears on front-wheel drive systems.

Differential and final drive combination

Differential

The differential is a special combination of gears, which allows the driven wheels of a vehicle to rotate at different speeds. When a car makes a turn, the outer wheel has to travel a greater distance than the inner, and hence must rotate at a faster speed. If this did not happen, the drive would break.

The differential can be called a torque equalizer

Driveshafts

Two driveshafts are used to pass the drive from the outputs of the final drive to each wheel. Each driveshaft contains two constant-velocity joints. These joints are covered with a rubber boot to keep out water and dirt.

This shaft transmits drive to the wheels

Propshaft

On rear-wheel drive vehicles, the drive has to be transferred from the gearbox output to the final drive and differential unit in the rear axle. The propshaft, short for propeller shaft, is a hollow tube with a universal joint at each end. If removed, the universal joints (UJs) must be aligned correctly. A UJ is like a cross with a bearing on each leg. It allows drive to be transmitted through an angle. This is to allow for suspension movement.

This shaft transmits drive to the final drive

Read the last few pages again and note down FIVE bullet points here:

Constant-Velocity Joint

The constant-velocity joint is a bit like a UJ. It is used on front-wheel drive driveshafts. It allows a smooth, constant velocity drive to be passed through, even when the suspension moves up and down and the steering moves side to side.

CV joints allow for this movement

Summary

The gearbox is clearly a key part of the transmission system. However, it must work in conjunction with other parts. All should be operating correctly for optimum performance.

Gearbox in use[2]

| KC | Describe the requirements of a constant velocity joint. |

Notes

Introduction

A transmission system gearbox is required because the power of an engine consists of speed and torque. Torque is the twisting force of the engine's crankshaft and speed refers to its rate of rotation. The transmission can adjust the proportions of torque and speed delivered from the engine to the driveshafts. When torque is increased, speed decreases and when speed is increased, the torque decreases. The transmission also reverses the drive and provides a neutral position when required.

Varying speeds make a gearbox essential!

Types of Gear

Helical gears are used for almost all modern gearboxes. They run more smoothly and operate more quietly. Earlier "sliding mesh" gearboxes used straight-cut gears, as these were easier to manufacture. Helical gears do produce some sideways force when operating, but this is dealt with by using thrust bearings.

Straight-cut and helical gears

Gearbox

For most light vehicles, a gearbox has five forward gears and one reverse gear. It is used to allow operation of the vehicle through a suitable range of speeds and torque. A manual gearbox needs a clutch to disconnect the engine crankshaft from the gearbox while changing gears. The driver changes gears by moving a lever, which is connected to the box by a mechanical linkage.

Modern Ford gearbox[2]

Power, Speed, and Torque

The gearbox converts the engine power by a system of gears, providing different ratios between the engine and the wheels. When the vehicle starts to move, the gearbox is placed in first, or low gear. This produces high torque but low wheel speed. As the car speeds up, the next higher gear is selected. With each higher gear, the output turns faster but with less torque.

Pontiac six-speed gear selector

Top Gears

Fourth gear on most rear-wheel drive light vehicles is called direct drive because there is no gear reduction in the gearbox. In other words, the gear ratio is 1:1. The output of the gearbox turns at the same speed as the crankshaft. For front-wheel drive vehicles, the ratio can be 1:1 or slightly different. Most modern light vehicles now have a fifth gear. This can be thought of as a kind of overdrive because the output always turns faster than the engine crankshaft.

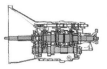

Fourth gear is often 'straight through'[1]

Gearbox Input

Power travels into the gearbox via the input shaft. A gear at the end of this shaft drives a gear on another shaft called the countershaft or layshaft. A number of gears of various sizes are mounted on the layshaft. These gears drive other gears on a third motion shaft known as the output shaft.

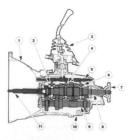

Sectioned view of a gearbox[1]

Sliding Mesh

Older vehicles used sliding-mesh gearboxes. With these gearboxes, the cogs moved in and out of contact with each other. Gear changing was, therefore, a skill that took time to master! These have now been replaced by constant-mesh gearboxes.

Gearbox basic operation

Constant Mesh

The modern gearbox still produces various gear ratios by engaging different combinations of gears. However, the gears are constantly in mesh. For reverse, an extra gear called an idler operates between the countershaft and the output shaft. It turns the output shaft in the opposite direction to the input shaft.

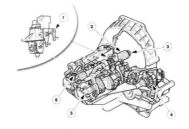

FWD gearbox (transaxle)[1]

Power Flow (RWD)

Note how in each case, with the exception of reverse, the gears do not move. This is why this type of gearbox has become known as constant mesh. In other words, the gears are running in mesh with each other at all times.

Click to see different gear power flows

Power Flow (FWD)

In constant mesh boxes, dog clutches are used to select which gears will be locked to the output shaft. These clutches, which are moved by selector levers, incorporate synchromesh mechanisms.

Summary

A manual gearbox allows the driver to select the gear appropriate to the driving conditions. Low gears produce low speed but high torque; high gears produce higher speed but lower torque.

Gearbox in use!

Read the last few pages again and note down FIVE bullet points here:

Introduction

There is a wide range of gearboxes in use. However, although the internal components differ, the principles remain the same. The examples in this section are, therefore, useful for learning the way in which any gearbox works.

Gearbox components[1]

Input Shaft

The input shaft transmits the torque from the clutch, via the countershaft, to the transmission output shaft. It runs inside a bearing at the front and has an internal bearing, which runs on the mainshaft, at the rear. The input shaft carries the countershaft driving gear and the synchronizer teeth and cone for fourth gear.

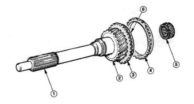

Details of the input shaft[1]

Mainshaft or Output Shaft

The mainshaft is mounted in the transmission housing at the rear and the input shaft at the front. This shaft carries all the main forward gears, the selectors, and the clutches. All the gears run on needle roller bearings. The gears run freely unless selected by one of the synchronizer clutches.

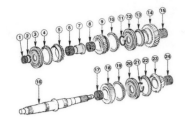

Details of the mainshaft.

Countershaft

The countershaft is sometimes called a layshaft. It is usually a solid shaft containing four or more gears. Drive is passed from here to the output shaft in all gears except fourth. The countershaft runs in bearings, fitted in the transmission case, at the front and rear.

Details of the countershaft[1]

Reverse Idler Gear

An extra gear has to be engaged to reverse the direction of the drive. A low ratio is used for reverse, even lower than first gear in many cases. The reverse idler connects the reverse gear to the countershaft.

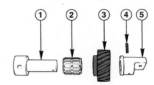

Details of the reverse gear idler[1]

Selector Mechanism

An interlock is used on all gearboxes to prevent more then one gear from being selected at any one time. If this were not prevented, the gearbox would lock, as the gears would be trying to turn the output at two different speeds – at the same time. The selectors are U-shaped devices that move the synchronizers.

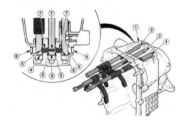

Details of the selector mechanism[1]

Selector and Synchronizer

Most gearboxes have three synchronizers. Their task is to bring the chosen gear to the correct speed for easy selection. The unit consists of cone clutches to synchronize speed, and dog clutches to connect the drive.

Details of the selector and synchronizer[1]

Transmission Fluid

The transmission fluid must meet the following requirements:

Viscosity must be largely unaffected by temperature

High aging resistance (gearboxes are usually filled for life)

Minimal tendency to foaming

Compatibility with different sealing materials

Only the specified transmission fluid should be used when topping off or filling after dismantling and reassembly. Otherwise, bearing and tooth-flank damage can occur.

A wide range of lubricants is available

Overdrive

On earlier vehicles, a four-speed gearbox was the norm. Further improvements in operation could be gained by fitting an overdrive. This was mounted on the output of the gearbox (RWD). In fourth gear, the drive ratio is usually 1:1. Overdrive would allow the output to rotate faster than the input, hence the name. Most gearboxes now incorporate a fifth gear, which is effectively an overdrive but does not form a separate unit.

Early overdrive unit in position

Read the last few pages again and note down FIVE bullet points here:

Summary

The transmission gearbox on all modern cars is a sophisticated component. However, the principle of operation does not change because it is based on simple gear ratios and clutch operation. Most current gearboxes are five speed, constant mesh, and use helical gears.

Nascar[2]

KC

State a typical ratio AND describe the process of engaging reverse gear.

State FOUR requirements of transmission fluid.

Introduction

On all modern gearboxes, the selection of different ratios is achieved by locking gears to the mainshaft. A synchromesh and clutch mechanism does this when moved by a selector fork. The selector fork is moved by a rod, or rail, which in turn is moved by the external mechanism and the gearstick.

Easy gear changing improves comfort[2]

Notes

Single Rail System

To save space, some manufacturers use a single selector shaft. This means the shaft has to twist and move lengthways. The twisting allows a finger to make contact with different selector forks. The lengthways movement pushes the synchronizers into position. All of the selector forks are fitted on the same shaft.

Gear shift or selector fork[1]

Two-Rail System

On a two-shaft system, the main selector shaft often operates the first/second gear selector fork. An auxiliary shaft operates the third/fourth selector fork.

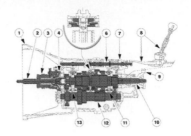

Double selector shaft[1]

Three-Rail System

The three-rail, or three-shaft system, is similar to the two-shaft type. However, each shaft can be moved lengthways. In turn, the shafts will move the first/second, third/fourth, or fifth/reverse forks.

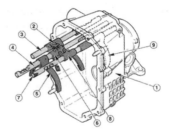

Triple selector shaft[1]

External Linkages

A common external linkage is shown here. Movement of the shift lever is transferred to the gearbox by a shift rod. The rod will only move to select reverse gear when the lock sleeve is lifted. This prevents accidental selection of reverse gear.

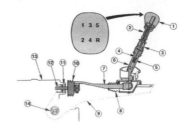

Rod operated shift mechanism[1]

Cable System

A recent development is the cable shift mechanism. The advantage of this system is that the shift lever does not have to be fixed to the gearbox or in a set position. This allows designers more freedom.

Ford cable change[2]

Detent Mechanism

A detent mechanism is used to hold the selected gear in mesh. In most cases, this is just a simple ball and spring acting on the selector shaft(s). A gearbox with the detent mechanisms highlighted is shown here.

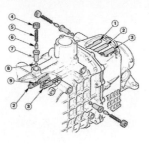

Ball and spring detent[1]

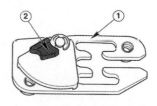

Gate and reverse gear lock[1]

Interlocks

Gear selection interlocks are a vital part of a gearbox. They prevent more than one gear from being engaged at any one time. When any selector clutch is in mesh, the interlock will not allow the remaining selectors to change position. As the main selector shaft is turned by side-to-side movement of the gear stick, the gate restricts the movement. The locking plate, shown as number 15, will only allow one shaft to be moved at a time. Because the gate restricts the movement, selection of more than one gear is prevented.

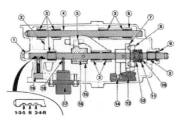

Gearshift mechanism[1]

Sliding Plunger Interlock

When three rails are used to select the gears, plungers or locking pins can be used. These lock the two remaining rails when one has moved. In the neutral position, each of the rails is free to move. When one rail (rod or shaft) has moved, the pins move into the locking notch, preventing the other rails from moving.

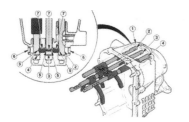

Plunger type interlock[1]

Read the last few pages again and note down FIVE bullet points here:

Summary

Gear selection must be a simple process for the driver. In order to facilitate changing, a number of mechanical components are needed. The external shift mechanism must transfer movement to the internal components. The internal mechanism must only allow selection of one gear at a time by use of an interlock. A detent system helps to hold the selected gear in place.

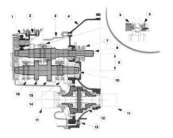

Design features of a transaxle[1]

KC　　State the advantage of a cable shift mechanism.

Introduction

A synchromesh mechanism is needed because the teeth of dog clutches clash if they meet at different speeds. Shown here is part of a synchronizer. The dog clutch and cone clutch are highlighted. A synchromesh system synchronizes the speed of two shafts before the dog clutches are meshed – hence the name.

Notes

Part of a synchronizer[1]

Synchromesh

The system works like a friction-type cone clutch. The collar is in two parts and contains an outer toothed ring, which is spring loaded to sit centrally on the synchromesh hub. When the outer ring, or synchronizer sleeve, is made to move by the action of the selector mechanism, the cone clutch is also moved because of the blocker bars.

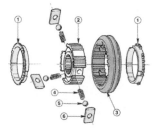

Synchronizer components[1]

Neutral Position

In the neutral position, the shift ring and blocker bars are centralized. There is no connection between the shift ring and the gear wheel. The gear wheel can turn freely on the shaft.

Synchronizer in neutral[1]

Synchronizing Position

When the shift fork is moved by the driver, the shift ring is slid toward the gear wheel. In the process, the shift ring carries three blocker bars, which move the synchronizer ring axially and press it onto the friction surface (cone clutch) of the gear wheel. As long as there is a difference in speed, the shift ring cannot move any further. This is because the frictional force turns the synchronizer ring, causing the tooth flanks to rest on the side of the synchronizer body.

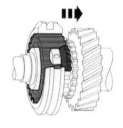

Synchronizer synchronizing[1]

Shift Position

Once the shift ring and gear are turning at the same speed, circumferential force no longer acts on them. The force still acting on the shift ring turns it until it slides onto the teeth of the gear wheel. The gear wheel is now locked to its shaft.

Synchronizer locked[1]

Synchronizer Movement

This animation shows the three stages of engagement:

Neutral

Synchronizing

Shift position

The system ensures that shifting gear is easy and that damage does not occur to the teeth.

Click the buttons to move the synchronizer

Read the last few pages again and note down **FIVE bullet points here:**

Reverse Gear

An extra shaft carries the reverse gear cog. Because reverse gears is selected with the car at a stop and low engine speed, some earlier gearboxes did not have a synchronizer on reverse. However, many modern boxes now include this feature.

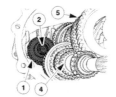

Reverse gear in position[1]

Summary

For two rotating shafts to mesh using a dog clutch, they should ideally be rotating at the same speed. Early motorists had to be skilled in achieving this through a process known as double-clutching. However, all modern gearboxes make life much easier for us by the use of synchromesh systems!

Synchromesh components

KC   Explain why reverse gear may not have synchromesh.

Introduction

Rear-wheel drive cars usually have the engine mounted lengthways in the car. The gearbox is mounted on the back of the engine in the same direction. It passes the drive via a propshaft to the rear axle. Front-wheel drive cars usually have the engine mounted transversely (sideways). The gearbox fits on the back of the engine but then straight gears pass the drive, via the final drive, to the driveshaft and wheels.

Lincoln LS
Sports[2]

Notes

Front-Wheel Drive (FWD)

Most front-wheel drive cars have a transmission system where the gearbox and final drive are combined. This is often described as a transaxle. The unit shown here is a five-speed box.

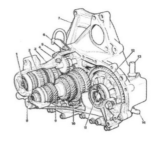

Internal transaxle features

Example FWD Gearbox

The selector fork, synchronizer, and the helical gears can be seen in this cutaway gearbox. The gears, as with all modern boxes, are in constant mesh. The correct lubricant is essential for these gearboxes. Damage will occur if the wrong type is used.

Cable change FWD gearbox (Ford)

FWD Gearbox Mountings

Front-wheel drive transmission gearboxes are solid-mounted on the engine. They are secured to the vehicle body or chassis with rubber mountings. This reduces noise and vibration for the passengers.

Rubber mountings reduce vibration

Speedometer Drive

The drive for the speedometer is taken from the gearbox output shaft on most vehicles. This shaft rotates at a speed proportional to road speed. Some manufacturers still use speedometer cables but many now opt for speed sensors, which provide a signal for an electronic gauge.

Speed sensor and cable connection

Rear-Wheel Drive (RWD)

Rear-wheel drive gearboxes do not usually contain final drive components. The exception is on four-wheel drive vehicles. The gearbox casing attaches to a bell housing, which bolts to the engine and covers the clutch. Larger vehicles use larger gearboxes because of the extra strength required. The operating principles are the same for all types.

Volvo transverse engine 4WD[2]

Example RWD Gearbox

General Motors use this box in the "Chevy Crew Cab." The gearbox is made by ZF. It is a six-speed manual transmission with the shift lever acting directly. Gearboxes, where the shift lever acts via a linkage, are often described as indirect or remote operated.

RWD gearbox[2]

RWD Gearbox Mountings

Rear-wheel drive transmission gearboxes are solid-mounted on the engine. They are secured to the vehicle body or chassis with rubber mountings. Usually a cross-member is fitted at the rear to support the weight. Rubber mountings reduce noise and vibration for the passengers.

Rubber mountings reduce noise

Reverse Light Switch

Most reverse light switches are simple on/off types. The switch body is fitted in the side of the gearbox casing. The toggle of the switch is moved by a selector shaft or other component when reverse gear is engaged.

Switch positions...[1]

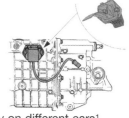

Vary on different cars[1]

Transmission Gearbox

This animation shows the operation of a front-wheel drive transmission system.

Gearbox operation

Summary

The gearbox is the main transmission component. Transmission is a general term used to describe all of the components required to transmit power from the engine to the wheels. The requirement is to convert the power from the relatively high velocity and low torque of the engine crankshaft to the usually lower speed and higher torque needed at the wheels. FWD and RWD gearboxes may look different but their operating principles are the same. Automatic transmission is another story.

Automatic transmission gearbox

Read the last few pages again and note down FIVE bullet points here:

KC   Describe how rear-wheel drive gearboxes are mounted to the engine and vehicle

Safety First

Before carrying out any service or repair work, refer to all appropriate health and safety guidelines. Always follow all safety procedures and observe safety precautions when working on vehicles. Some specific hazards are listed in this section. General safety advice is also included.

Be smart, be safe[2]

Notes

Asbestos

Many types of brake-lining material and friction discs contain asbestos fibers. Always follow safety precautions when handling asbestos.

Breathing mask in use

Running Engines

Running engines are sometimes needed for diagnostics and system checks. A running engine presents two hazards: The first is the risk from rotating components and the second from the accumulation of exhaust gas in the workshop. Remain aware of rotating parts such as the fan, belt, and pulleys in the areas where you are likely to be working.

Be aware of moving parts

Electrically Driven Fans

An electrically driven fan is switched on automatically when the temperature of the coolant in the radiator rises above the switch operating temperature. This can occur even when the ignition is switched off. When performing diagnostic tests, always keep fingers out of the fan cowl and always remove the battery ground cable when the engine does not need to be running.

Fans can start at any time

Exhaust Emissions

When running an engine, it is important to prevent the build-up of exhaust gas in the workshop. Use extraction equipment or provide good ventilation.

Extraction equipment

Hot Components

When used for prolonged periods, vehicle components can become very hot. In particular, take care not to touch the exhaust when working under the vehicle or on the engine.

Be aware of hot exhausts

Protective Clothing

Overalls should ideally be worn at all times. This protects your clothes as well as your skin. Gloves, goggles, breathing masks, hats, and strong footwear may also be necessary.

Personal protective equipment in use

Working Below Vehicles

There are a number of hazards to avoid when working under vehicles. One is the risk of hitting your head, which can obviously cause injury. Another risk is the possibility of getting rust and dirt in the eyes. Avoid these problems by wearing a bump cap and goggles whenever working below vehicles. The vehicle must always be supported safely before working underneath or alongside it.

Car on a ramp

Heavy Loads

The lifting and moving of heavy loads also pose risks. Many vehicle components fall into this category. Always tackle these tasks in an appropriate manner by ensuring the use of the recommended lifting equipment. Ask for assistance if necessary. Even some propshafts can be difficult to handle.

Gearbox[2]

Jacking and Supporting

Only use the recommended jacking and support points when lifting a vehicle. Refer to the manufacturer's instructions if unsure. Make sure that the jack and support stands, which must be used at all times, have an appropriate safe working load (SWL).

Jacking point

Skin Contact

When servicing vehicle systems avoid skin contact with new and used engine oils. Use barrier cream or non-porous gloves. Be careful with hot oil, particularly when carrying out oil draining operations. Never keep oily rags in overalls or other pockets and change out of oil-contaminated clothing as soon as reasonably possible.

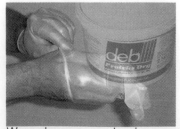
Wear gloves or use barrier cream

Caution-Attention-Achtung!

All types of fuel – and particularly the vapors – are highly flammable. They can be ignited from a number of sources. Any exposed flame, a short circuit, a cigarette, or, under the right conditions, even a hot object will start a fire.

Take care!

Electrical Sparks

Electrical sparks are the most common cause of vehicle fires in the workshop. These can occur during the connection and removal of electrical terminals. Sparks also occur when the engine is cranked with the ignition on and the spark plugs removed. Disconnect the coil or connect the HT cables directly to ground to prevent this.

Sparks from the battery lead

Short Circuits

If a wire or tool is allowed to join the battery's positive connection to the negative connection, a serious short circuit will result. A wire would become extremely hot and, in addition to the obvious fire risk, would burn through whatever part of your body it was touching. This demonstration shown here was carried out under the supervision of highly trained fire experts. Do NOT attempt to copy it. The same results occur if shorts are made on the vehicle. Exercise caution.

Do NOT try this!

Original Equipment

In consideration of other people's property, always be careful to use approved parts. Original equipment manufacturer's (OEM) parts may be required to meet safety regulations.

Use good quality transmission parts[2]

Refrigerant

Refrigerant used in air conditioning systems is dangerous. If it comes in contact with the skin, it produces severe frostbite. Wear protective goggles and gloves at all times. Use gloves designed for the purpose; leather or fabric gloves are NOT suitable. If refrigerant is exposed to open flames or hot surfaces, it produces toxic gases. Always ensure adequate ventilation when working on air-conditioning systems.

Air conditioning system connections

Read the last few pages again and note down FIVE bullet points here:

Pressurized Cooling Systems

If work has to be carried out on the vehicle heater or the cooling system, there is a risk of scalding. The coolant is run at pressure higher than atmospheric. If the cap is removed when hot, the coolant can boil instantly, ejecting boiling water and steam.

Heater radiator

Rotating Driveline Components

The Ferrari shown here was test driven on a rolling road. It was driven at well in excess of 100 mph! Note how important it is to ensure that all driveline components are in good order.

Test on a rolling road

Transmission Wind Up

On four-wheel drive vehicles, it is possible for the transmission to "wind up" when the front and rear axles are locked together. This is because the two axles may run at slightly different speeds. When on rough ground it is not a problem because the bouncing and movement allows the tires to slip. On hard surfaces, however, a twist or "wind-up" of components such as driveshafts occurs. When the vehicle is jacked up, the transmission can unwind suddenly causing serious injury. This does not occur on vehicles with an unlocked center differential or a viscous drive.

Simulation of wind-up

Scheduled Servicing

Scheduled service requirements are often quite simple but nonetheless important. Systems should be checked for correct operation. Adjustments, repairs, or replacements are then made if required. The servicing requirements for the driveshafts are limited but equally important.

All systems need some maintenance[2]

Notes

Non-Routine Work

When carrying out routine maintenance, some non-routine work may be found. This should be reported to the driver or owner of the vehicle before expensive repairs are carried out.

Transmission oil leak

Workshop Tasks

Worksheets for routine maintenance of the system are included in this program. Refer to the safety precautions in the Health and Safety sections before carrying out any practical work on vehicles. The worksheets can be printed and used as part of a practical training program. They give general instructions only and should therefore be used together with a manufacturer's workshop manual. Other good sources of information will also be required.

Refer to other sources of data as necessary

Worksheet

Service transmission system.

The service requirements for the transmission system are straightforward. However, it is still important that the work be carried out regularly and with care. The task mostly involves a quick check of the system and topping off the oils. Note that you should always check manufacturer's data for the correct lubricant type.

Read the last few pages again and note down FIVE bullet points here:

Checking the transmission data

Gearbox Service

To gain access to the gearbox and other components, jack up and support the vehicle or raise it on a hoist. Remove the plug in the side of the gearbox. This will require a square or a hexagonal tool. Note that two plugs are used, one to drain the oil at the bottom and the upper one for filling up. If the oil is not at the bottom of the upper opening, use a pump or squeeze bottle to top off. Do this until the oil just runs out of the hole. Refit the plug securely but do not overtighten and strip the threads.

Filling the gearbox oil

Transmission Service

If appropriate, repeat the previous procedure for the overdrive unit and final drive assemblies. Clean the areas around the plugs, gaskets, and any seals by wiping with a cloth. Road test the vehicle and then check for leaks. Double check that any plugs and covers, which were removed, have been securely replaced. Lower the vehicle to the ground.

General inspection of the transmission system

Summary

This transmission service task will normally be carried out as part of a general service call. If the need for other work (such as to repair a serious leak) is noticed, this should be reported to the customer.

Small oil leak

Serious oil leak

Notes

Regular Checks

Regular servicing is vital for a customer's safety. Carry out checks at all services and report your findings to the customer. Advise customers if anything will need attention before the next scheduled service interval.

Explain any unusual conditions to the customer

Vehicle Condition

Respect your customer's vehicle and take precautions to keep it clean. Repairing or checking some systems is likely to involve you working under the vehicle and then sitting in the driver's seat. Use seat covers and ensure that the steering wheel is clean when you have finished.

Seat covers and mats in use

Keep Customers Informed

Some customers like to know details of what work has been done to their vehicle – and they have every right to know! Here, an oil leak is being shown to the car's owner. The customer appreciated having the situation explained.

A small problem now, but it may get worse

Test Drives

Take the customer on a test drive if necessary. It is a useful way of helping them to describe problems to you. Alternatively, they could drive and demonstrate what is concerning them. Simple problems like wheel-bearing noise can be diagnosed easily in this way.

Test drive with the customer if necessary

Shifting

Should a customer express concern about gear changing (shifting), carry out a few simple checks before removing the transmission. With the engine stationary, check that the clutch pedal and gear lever can move freely. Check for correct fitment of mats, rubber gaiters, and sound-damping material. Look for play and wear in the gear lever guide and engagement of the shift rod bolt in the universal joint. With the engine running, check for correct clutch disengagement.

Changing gears

Transmission Noises

Should a customer express concern about transmission noises, a few simple checks should be carried out before doing any repairs. Check that the gaiters and the sound-damping material are fitted correctly on the gear lever. Make sure that the transmission is correctly filled with lubricant.

Gear change gaiter

Expensive Work

If a problem with the transmission system requires replacement or repair of the gearbox, this will result in a significant cost to the customer. Make sure you keep the customer informed at all times.

New gearbox in position

Summary

A customer who is kept informed and treated with respect will return and keep you in a job! Explain things to a customer when asked – it will be appreciated.

Customers will return if they get good service

Read the last few pages again and note down FIVE bullet points here:

Notes

Introduction

System performance checks are routine activities that occur during all servicing work. They start at pre-delivery and continue for all scheduled service intervals.

Systems need checking regularly[2]

Quick Checks

Quick checks must be thorough and must look for incorrect operation or adjustment and the first signs of deterioration. Detailed diagnostic procedures may be required to identify faulty components. Always refer to the manufacturer's data where necessary.

Manufacturer's data

Workshop Tasks

Worksheets for checking the performance of the system are included in this program. Refer to the safety precautions in the Health and Safety sections before carrying out any practical work on vehicles. The worksheets can be printed and used as part of a practical training program. They give general instructions only. Therefore, they should be used together with a manufacturer's workshop manual or some other good source of information.

Refer to other sources of data as necessary

Worksheet

Check transmission operation.

As a preliminary procedure, perform a visual inspection as part of the diagnostic routine prior to a road test and note anything that does not look right. Check the tire pressures and look for fluid leaks, loose parts, and bright spots where components may be rubbing against each other. Check the trunk for unusual loads. Finally, check all of the transmission oil levels.

Transmission components

Road Test

Establish a route that will be used for all diagnosis road tests. This allows you to get to know what is normal and what is not! The roads selected should have reasonably smooth sections. Road test the vehicle and check any unusual condition by reproducing it several times. Normally the whole transmission system will be road tested. However, just the issues relating to the gearbox will be examined in detail here.

Road testing a vehicle

Road Test Conditions

Use ALL the gears during the test and recreate the following conditions:

Normal driving speeds of 20 to 80-km/h (15 to 50 mph) with light acceleration

Harder acceleration and deceleration

Low speed and high speed

Over-run or coast down

Coasting with the clutch pedal down or gear lever in neutral and engine idling

Check for any unusual vibrations from the gear lever

Road Test Symptoms

Under the road test conditions, stated previously, check for the following gearbox symptoms:

Rumbling noises - may indicate worn bearings

Whining noises - may indicate worn or incorrectly set gears

Crunching noises when changing gear - may indicate synchronizer problems

Jumping out of gear - may indicate a detent or synchronizer problem

Knocking at low speed - may indicate that a gear is chipped

Gear   Bearing   Synchronizer   Detent

Transmission Inspection

After the road test, continue to inspect the vehicle after raising it on a hoist. In particular, look for oil leaks and loose mountings. Check the security and condition of the gear-change mechanism. After a thorough test, you may need to tell the customer that the problem is in the gearbox, but that you will have to remove it before a detailed diagnosis is possible. On older vehicles, many workshops will recommend that the gearbox be replaced. This allows accurate pricing for the customer and, assuming quality parts are used, a guarantee of reliability.

Inspecting the transmission

Worksheet

Check gear-change operation and adjust linkage.

Raise the vehicle on a hoist or use a jack and stands as required. Check and top off all transmission fluid levels. Linkages vary from a single rod to cable operation.

Gear change linkage   Cable change gearbox[2]

Read the last few pages again and note down FIVE bullet points here:

Gear-Change Operation

Using a lever, check rubber transmission mountings for excessive movement. Move the gear-change linkage – with help from an assistant, if necessary – and check for damage or wear. Make sure each gear is selected during the checking process.

Checking gearbox mountings

Gear-Linkage Adjustment

If adjustment is required, refer to the manufacturer's specific recommendations. Some require a special tool; others recommend measurements that should be taken and the lengths of threaded rods to be set. If a linkage has to be removed for repair work, mark it carefully first. Use small scratches or dot punch marks. Complete the checks or adjustment routines with a road test.

Adjustment information

Summary

Transmission components make a contribution toward the safety of the vehicle. Therefore, system performance checks are important. Cars are operated at high speeds, and sudden breakdowns can be dangerous. It is important that systems function correctly at all times.

Busy traffic!

Introduction

Some special test equipment is used when working with gearbox components. Remember, you should always refer to the manufacturer's instructions appropriate to the equipment you are using.

Refer to the manufacturer's instructions

Notes

Dial Test Gauge

A dial test gauge or dial test indicator (DTI) is a useful piece of measuring equipment. It is usually used in conjunction with a magnetic stand. As the needle is moved, the dial, via a series of accurate gears, indicates the distance traveled. The graduations are either hundredths of a millimeter or thousandths of an inch.

DTI and stand

Torque Wrench

A good torque wrench is an essential piece of equipment. Many types are available but all work on a similar principle. Most are set by adjusting a screwed cylinder, which forms part of the handle. An important point to remember is that, as with any measuring tool, regular calibration is essential to ensure that it remains accurate.

Torque wrench in use

Preload Torque Gauge

A type of torque equipment is used to test the turning torque of some components. A good example of this is shown here. The turning torque of the final drive pinion is used to set the pinion bearing preload on some vehicles.

Testing turning torque[1]

Read the last few pages again and note down FIVE bullet points here:

Accuracy

To ensure that measuring equipment remains accurate, there are just two simple guidelines:

Look after the kit – test equipment thrown on the floor will not be accurate.

Ensure that instruments are calibrated regularly – this means being checked against known-good equipment.

Micrometer in use

Notes

Introduction

The secret to finding faults is to have a good knowledge of the system and to work in a logical way. Use manufacturer's data and recommended procedures. This section includes general faultfinding procedures for gearbox work.

Check data before starting work

Symptoms and Faults

Remember that a symptom is the observed result of a fault. Each of the next few screens states a common symptom and possible faults. These are diagnosed as the vehicle is being driven in most cases. It is important to note that faults in one system can produce symptoms that may appear to be caused by another. Also, note that the stated symptoms and faults will vary across different vehicles and systems.

Symptoms are the result of faults

Noise in a Particular Gear (With Engine Running)

Faults that are possible causes of this symptom are:

Damaged gear teeth

Worn bearing

Incorrectly adjusted selection mechanism

Chipped gear tooth

Noise in Neutral (With Engine Running)

Faults that are possible causes of this symptom are:

Gearbox input-shaft bearings are worn (goes away when clutch is pushed down)

Lack of lubricating oil

Clutch-release bearing worn (gets worse when clutch is pushed down)

Input shaft bearing

Difficult to Engage Gears

Faults that are possible causes of this symptom are:

Clutch not releasing correctly

Gear linkage worn or not adjusted correctly

Work synchromesh units

Lack of lubrication

Gear A selected   Neutral   Gear B selected

Jumps out of Gear

Faults that are possible causes of this symptom are:

Gear linkage worn or not adjusted correctly

Worn selector forks

Detent not working

Weak synchromesh units

 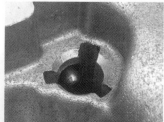

Detent...   Mechanism

Vibration

Faults that are possible causes of this symptom are:

Lack of lubrication

Worn bearings

Mountings loose

Gearbox mounting

Oil Leaks

Faults that are possible causes of this symptom are:

Gaskets leaking

Worn oil seals

Oil seal

Systematic Testing

Working through a logical and systematic procedure for testing a system is the only reliable way to diagnose a problem. Use these six stages of faultfinding as a guide.

Stages of faultfinding

Faultfinding Procedure

As an example of how the stages are applied, assume the reported symptom is that the car jumps out of third and fourth gear when under load. The recommended procedure is outlined on the next five screens.

Check the latest data

Verify the Fault

Road test the car, with the customer if possible, to recreate the symptoms. Remember, it is not that you don't believe the customer! It is often difficult for a driver to describe symptoms without technical knowledge. It is particularly difficult to narrow down sources of noise! Jumping out of gear usually occurs on acceleration or deceleration.

Road test

Collect Further Information

Make sure, during the road test, that you drive the car through a variety of conditions. Talk to the customer. Ask, for example, if the problem started suddenly or gradually. Check the feel of the gearshift as it is moved. Look under the car for oil leaks.

A quick check under the car

Evaluate the Evidence

Remember at this point to stop and think! If the problem developed slowly, it may suggest that a component such as a detent spring is wearing out. However, because the problem occurs in third AND fourth gear, you may be suspicious of the third/fourth selector or synchronizer.

Stop and think!

Carry Out Further Tests

After a road test, you should have an idea of what is causing the symptoms. Most faults of this type are internal to the gearbox. However, you should be sure before reporting this to the customer. Check the linkage and mountings as described earlier.

Checking the linkage

Fixing the Problem

The work required to fix this problem can vary from installing a new gearbox to replacing a broken detent spring. Refer to the manufacturer's data for specific procedures.

A new gearbox being fitted!

Only a new spring needed!

Check All Systems

It is possible, when fixing one fault, to accidentally cause a new problem. It is also possible that another fault exists, and it may appear to the customer that you have caused it! For both of these reasons, check that ALL systems work correctly after any repairs have been carried out.

A quick check of all systems

Read the last few pages again and note down FIVE bullet points here:

Summary

Faultfinding work is rewarding – when you find the fault! Remember to always work in a logical way. The stages of faultfinding can be applied to all systems on the vehicle, complex or simple.

Job finished

Module 5. Component Inspection and Repair
Section 1. Tools and Equipment

Introduction

Components will usually be removed, inspected, and repaired or replaced when a defect has been diagnosed. Other components are replaced, or stripped and cleaned, at scheduled mileage or time intervals. Refer to the Routine Maintenance section for details on these items.

Good tools and equipment are important5

Procedures

The descriptions provided in this section deal with the components for individual replacement rather than as a part of other work. Always refer to a workshop manual before starting work. You will also need to look for the recommended procedure, special tools, materials, tightening sequences, and torque settings. Some general and specific tools and pieces of equipment are described on the following screens.

Refer to data as required

General Toolkit

General tools and equipment will be required for most tasks. As your career develops, you will build a collection of tools and equipment. Look after your tools and they will look after you!

Snap-on tools

Soft Hammers

These tools allow you to pound hard without causing damage. They are ideal for working on gearboxes. Some types are made of special hard plastics whereas some are copper/hide mallets. This type has a copper insert on one side and a hide or leather insert on the other. It is still possible to cause damage, however, so you must still be careful!

Some hammers contain metal shot to give a 'dead blow'[5]

Support Bars

When removing gearboxes from some vehicles, it is necessary to support the engine. This is because the engine and gearbox (on front-wheel drive vehicles, in particular) share the same mountings. Most support equipment is a simple steel frame that fits across two support points such as suspension mounts. A chain or cable is connected to the engine and its tension is adjusted.

Engine support equipment

Jacks and Stands

Most jacks are simple hydraulic devices. Remember to make sure the safe working load (SWL) is not exceeded. Ensure that any problems with equipment such as this are reported immediately. Axle stands must always be placed under the vehicle supporting the weight – before work is carried out.

Use stands after jacking a vehicle

Ramps and Hoists

Many ramps or hoists are available. These range from large four-post, wheel-free types to smaller single-post lifts. These items should be inspected regularly to ensure that they are safe.

Four-post lift in use

Transmission Jack

If a complete gearbox has to be removed, it is likely to be heavy! A transmission jack has attachments that allow you to support the gearbox and lower it safely. The equipment is hydraulically operated just like an ordinary jack. Often, the height can be set by using a foot pedal, which leaves both hands free for positioning the unit.

Transmission jacks are very useful

Read the last few pages again and note down FIVE bullet points here:

Bearing Puller

Removing some bearings can be difficult without a proper puller. For internal bearings, the tool has small legs and feet that hook under the bearing. A threaded section is tightened to pull out the bearing. External pullers hook over the outside of the bearing and a screwed thread is tightened against the shaft. These tools may be essential for gearbox work.

Internal and external bearing pullers[5]

Air Tools

The whole point of power tools is that they do the work so you don't have to! However, air guns produce a "hammer" action, and, because of this, impact sockets should be used. Normal sockets can shatter under this load. It is important to remember that air tools need lubricating from time to time. Air ratchets are very useful for removing or fitting nuts and bolts. However, it is possible to over-tighten if you are not careful. Air tools can be very powerful and will trap your hands! Take adequate precautions at all times.

These tools are very useful[5]

Slide Hammer

A slide hammer is a form of puller. It consists of a steel rod over which a heavy mass slides. The mass is "hammered" against a stop, thus applying a pulling action. The clamp end of the tool can screw either into, or onto, the component. Alternatively, puller legs with feet are used to grip under the sides of the component.

These tools are used for removing shafts[5]

Grease Gun

A grease gun is a simple device that pumps grease under pressure. A special connector fits onto a grease nipple. Some types are air-operated but the one shown here is a simple pump-action type.

Used mostly on older or heavy vehicles[5]

Workshop Tasks

Worksheets for removing, replacing, stripping, and rebuilding the system are included in this program. Refer to the safety precautions in the Health and Safety sections before carrying out any practical work on vehicles. The worksheets can be printed and used as part of a practical training program. They give general instructions only. Therefore, they should be used together with a manufacturer's workshop manual or some other good source of information.

Refer to other sources of data as necessary

Worksheet

Remove and refit transmission gearbox (transaxle type).

The procedure outlined here is generic and relates to a front-wheel drive vehicle. You should refer to specific manufacturer's data as required. The first task is to support the vehicle on a suitable hoist. Fit a car protection kit as required and disconnect the battery. Remember to hook up a memory keeper if necessary. Drain the gearbox oil.

Disconnect the battery ground

Gearbox Removal

Remove any ancillary components as necessary. This will allow easier access to the gearbox. For example, the exhaust may need to be removed. Mark the gear change linkage and then remove parts as required. Remove the minimum number of parts or remove the linkage as a complete unit where possible. This makes reinstalling a lot easier. On some vehicles, it is necessary to remove the suspension on one side to allow access to the gearbox, and for removal of the driveshafts. Remove the driveshafts from the final drive.

Gear change linkage   Removing the driveshafts

Engine Support

Remove the speedometer cable or speed sensor. Remove the reverse (back-up) light switch wires. Tie these components out of the way. Remove the starter motor if necessary. Use an engine support bar as required; remove mountings and cross members. Support the gearbox on a transmission jack if necessary and remove the gearbox or bell-housing bolts. Move the gearbox straight out of the clutch assembly, away from the vehicle, and place it on a suitable bench.

Speedometer connection   Mountings   Bell housing bolts   Gearbox being removed

Refitting the Gearbox

As usual – reinstallation is a reversal of the removal process! However, it is normal to strip and check the clutch assembly if the gearbox is removed. When the clutch assembly is refitted, make sure it is aligned correctly. This makes refitting the gearbox much easier. Remember to refill the gearbox with the correct lubricant and check that all fixings are tightened correctly. A road test is recommended to ensure correct operation when the job is completed.

Clutch aligned position   Refitting the gearbox   Securing the mounting bolts   Top off the oil

Worksheet

Remove and refit gear change mechanism.

This is a generic procedure for a rear-wheel drive vehicle. Refer to specific manufacturer's data as required. Disconnect the ground cable from the battery. On some cars, it will be necessary to remove the passenger's seat or driver's seat to gain access.

Removing the covers

Read the last few pages again and note down FIVE bullet points here:

Gear Linkage Removal

Remove the knob at the top of the gearshift. Most will unscrew but some are held with a small screw. Remove console covers, gaiters, and panels as necessary to gain access. Disconnect the shift-rod levers or unscrew the ball-joint cover as appropriate. Disconnect the electrical wiring for the overdrive switch (if fitted) and remove the gearshift.

Gear change mechanism

Refitting the Linkage

Place the gearshift in position and install the ball-joint cover or shift-rod levers. Adjust the linkage if necessary. Connect the overdrive electrical switch wiring (if fitted). Finally, reinstall the covers, panels, and other components as appropriate.

Refitting the gaiters

Introduction

The main inspections and measurements carried out to the system are included in this section. General inspections should take place at scheduled service intervals, and if problems have been reported. Specific inspection and measurement work, as described here, is only done when detailed repairs are carried out.

Inspections keep a good car in good order[2]

Workshop Tasks

Worksheets for inspections and measurement of the system are included in this section. Refer to the safety precautions in the Health and Safety sections before carrying out any practical work on vehicles. The worksheets can be printed and used as part of a practical training program. They give general instructions only. Therefore, they should be used along with a manufacturer's workshop manual or some other good source of information.

Refer to data as required

Worksheet

Inspect and measure gearbox components. Gearbox components and methods of removal vary considerably between manufacturers. This list is a general guide to the process of checking and measuring. For instructions on disassembly, refer to specific manufacturer's data.

Stripping the gearbox

Ball and Roller Bearings

Wash the bearings in a solvent and dry them. Rotate the inner and outer races. Listen for noises and feel for any tight spots. Replace them if a problem is suspected.

Input shaft bearing

Needle roller bearing

Main Gears and Mainshaft

Look for signs of wear and chipped teeth. Use a wire to check any oil passages. Check all areas for wear and damage. The mainshaft bearing surfaces can be measured with a micrometer and compared to data. Remember to check inside the bearings as well as the shaft.

Gear teeth

Layshaft/ Counter Gear Assembly

On many gearboxes, the layshaft/counter gear is a single assembly. The gears should be checked for wear and chipping; the bearing surfaces should be checked for wear and ovality using a micrometer.

Layshaft

Synchronizers

The main parts to check are the synchronizer cone clutches and the dog clutches. Also, check the grooves where the selector forks run for signs of wear. This is a moving component and is more likely to wear.

Selector and synchronizer mechanism

Reverse Gear and Shaft

Look for signs of wear and chipped teeth. Use a wire to check any oil passages. Check bearing surfaces on the shaft. Also, check the reverse gear-selector mechanism for signs of wear.

Idler shaft and reverse gear

Input Shaft Assembly

Look for signs of wear and chipped teeth on the main input gear. Use a wire to check any oil passages. Check the bearing surfaces and the oil seal. Seals are normally replaced as a matter of course if the gearbox is disassembled.

Gearbox input shaft

Read the last few pages again and note down FIVE bullet points here:

Selector Rods and Forks

Check for wear and signs of overheating, which may occur if the forks have been rubbing. This may occur if the driver holds the gearshift after a gear is selected.

Selectors

Detent and Interlock Mechanism

Make sure the detent balls and springs are in good order. Replace them if there's any doubt. The interlock mechanism should prevent two gears from being selected at the same time. Examine all components carefully for wear and correct operation.

Interlock components

Detent mechanism

Gearbox Casing and Other Components

Check the casing for cracks and porosity. Use new gaskets and seals when rebuilding. Any other parts such as the speedometer drive gear and the reverse light switch should be checked for security and correct operation.

Output oil seals

Speedometer drive gears

Summary

Some gearbox repairs can involve significant work. However, do not make any compromises. Keep your customers – and yourself – happy and safe.

Gearbox back together!

TOPIC: TRANSMISSION DRIVELINE

Module 1. Transmission Driveshafts
Section 1. Transmission

Introduction

Transmission is a general term used to describe all of the components required to transmit power from the engine to the wheels. The requirement is to convert the power from the relatively high velocity and low torque of the engine crankshaft to the variable, usually lower speed and higher torque needed at the wheels. This first section is a general introduction to the transmission system.

Transmission components are important[2]

Types of Transmission

The two basic types of transmissions use either a manual gearbox, in which the gears are selected by the driver, or an automatic gearbox, in which the gears are changed automatically. The other driveline components, with the exception of the clutch, are the same for automatic or manual systems.

Manual transmission

Automatic transmission

Front-Wheel Drive Transmission

Working from the engine to the wheels, the main components of a typical front-wheel drive transmission system are:

Clutch

Gearbox

Final drive

Differential

Driveshafts

Clutch | Gearbox | Final drive and differential | Driveshaft

Rear-Wheel Drive Transmission

Working from the engine to the wheels, the main components of a typical rear-wheel drive transmission system are:

Clutch

Gearbox

Propshaft

Final drive

Differential

Half shafts

Clutch | Gearbox | Final drive and differential | Propshaft

Clutch

Fitted between the engine and gearbox, the clutch allows the drive to be disconnected when the pedal is depressed. It allows a smooth take-up of drive and allows gears to be changed.

Clutch assembly

Manual Gearbox

A manual gearbox is a box full of gears of varying ratios. The ratio most suitable for the current driving conditions can be selected by the driver. Most boxes contain about thirteen gear cogs, which allow five forward gears and one reverse.

A box of gears!

Torque Converter

A torque converter is sometimes called a fluid flywheel (although the two differ slightly) and is used in conjunction with an automatic gearbox. It has two main parts. As the input section rotates, fluid pressure begins to act on the output section, which is made to rotate. As speed increases, a better drive is made. The drive, therefore, takes up automatically and smoothly.

Converter as part of a Ford CTX transmission[2]

Automatic Gearbox

As the name suggests, this is a gearbox that operates automatically. Most types contain special gear arrangements known as epicyclic gear trains. Some now use complicated electronic control, but the basic principle is that fluid pressure from a pump, which changes with road speed, is used to change the gears.

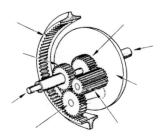

Epicyclic gears are often used in an 'auto-box'[1]

Final Drive

To produce the required torque at the road wheels, a fixed gear reduction from the high engine speed is required. The final drive consists of just two gears with a ratio of about 4:1. These are bevel gears on rear-wheel drive systems and normal gears on front-wheel drive vehicles.

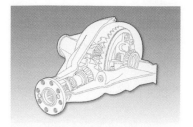

Differential and final drive combination

Differential

A differential is a special combination of gears, which allows the driven wheels of a vehicle to rotate at different speeds. Think of a car going around a turn. The outer wheel has to travel a greater distance, and hence must rotate at a faster speed than the inner wheel. Otherwise, the drive would 'wind up' and something would break.

The differential can be called a torque equalizer

Driveshafts

Two driveshafts are used to pass the drive from the outputs of the final drive to each wheel. Each driveshaft contains two constant-velocity joints. These joints are covered with a rubber boot to keep out water and dirt.

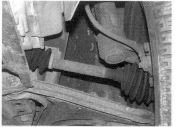

This shaft transmits drive to the wheels

Propshaft

On rear-wheel drive vehicles, the drive has to be transferred from the gearbox output to the final drive and differential unit in the rear axle. The propshaft, short for propeller shaft, is a hollow tube with a universal joint at each end. If removed, the universal joints (UJs) must be realigned correctly.

Read the last few pages again and note down FIVE bullet points here:

This shaft transmits drive to the final drive

Universal Joint

A universal joint is like a cross with a bearing on each leg. It allows drive to be transmitted through an angle. This is to allow for suspension movement.

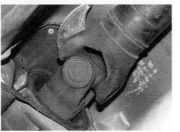

This is called a UJ

Constant-Velocity Joint

The constant-velocity (CV) joint is similar to a universal joint. It is used on front-wheel drive driveshafts. It allows a smooth, constant-velocity drive to be passed through, even when the suspension moves up and down and the steering moves from side to side.

CV joints allow for this movement

Summary

Driveline components are key parts of the transmission system. However, they must work in conjunction with other parts. All should be operating correctly for optimum performance.

Drive shafts in use[2]

KC	State the three main parts of a torque converter.

Introduction

Propshafts, with universal joints, are used on rear- or four-wheel drive vehicles. They transmit drive from the gearbox output to the final drive in the rear axle. Drive then continues through the final drive and differential via two half shafts to each rear wheel.

Propshaft

Notes

Main Shaft

A hollow steel tube is used for the main shaft. This is lightweight, but will still transfer considerable turning forces. It will also resist bending forces.

Section of a propshaft

Universal Joints (UJs)

Universal joints allow for the movement of the rear axle with the suspension, while the gearbox remains fixed. Two joints are used on most systems and must always be aligned correctly.

Details of a UJ

Variable Velocity

Because of the angle through which the drive is turned, a variation in speed results. This is caused because two arms of the universal joint rotate in one plane and two in another. The cross of the universal joint, therefore, has to change position twice on each revolution. However, this problem can be overcome by making sure the two universal joints are aligned correctly.

Speed variations would cause vibration

Universal Joint Alignment

If the two universal joints on a propshaft are aligned correctly, the variation in speed caused by the first can be canceled out by the second. However, the angles through which the shaft works must be equal. The main body of the propshaft will run with variable velocity but the output drive will be constant.

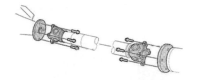

These joints are aligned correctly[1]

Universal Joint Bearings

The simplest and most common type of universal joint consists of a four-point cross, which is sometimes called a spider. Four needle-type roller bearings are fitted, one on each arm of the cross. Two bearings are held in the driver yoke and two in the driven yoke.

Details of a universal joint

Universal Joint Developments

Several types of universal joints have been used on vehicles. These developed from the simple Hooke-type joint, to the later cross-type, often known as a Hardy Spicer. Rubber joints are also used on some vehicles.

Hooke-type joint   Cross-type joint   Layrub joint   Donut joint

Rubber Couplings

The donut coupling has the advantage of being flexible and absorbing torsional shocks. It also will tend to reduce vibrations caused by other joints. Its other main advantage is that it allows some axial (back and forth) movement.

Donut coupling

Suspension Movement

As the suspension moves up and down, the length of the driveline changes slightly. As the rear wheels hit a bump, the axle moves upward. This tends to shorten the driveline. The splined sliding joint allows for this movement.

Change in driveline length

Sliding Joint

A sliding joint allows for axial movement. However, it will also transfer the rotational drive. Internal splines are used on the propshaft so that the external surface is smooth. This allows an oil seal to be fitted into the gearbox output casing.

A splined joint connects to the gearbox

Center Bearings

When long propshafts are used, there is a danger of vibration because the weight of the propshaft can cause it to sag slightly and therefore 'whip' (like a jumping rope) as it rotates. Most center bearings are standard ball bearings mounted in rubber.

A splined joint connects to the gearbox

Summary

Propshafts are used on rear- or four-wheel drive vehicles. They transmit drive from the gearbox output to the rear axle. Most propshafts contain two universal joints. A single joint produces rotational velocity variations, but these can be canceled out if the second joint is aligned correctly. Center bearings are used to prevent vibration due to propshaft whip.

A propshaft transfers drive from the gearbox to the rear axle[2]

Read the last few pages again and note down FIVE bullet points here:

KC   State the purpose of the splined joint on a propshaft.

Notes

Introduction

Driveshafts with constant-velocity joints transmit drive from the output of the final drive and differential to each front wheel. They must also allow for suspension and steering movements.

Driveshaft and CV joints

Constant-Velocity (CV) Joint

A constant-velocity joint is a universal joint; however, it is constructed so that the output rotational speed is the same as the input speed. The speed of rotation remains constant even as the suspension and steering move the joint.

Outer CV joint

Inner and Outer Joints

The inner and outer joints have to perform different tasks. The inner joint has to move in and out to take up the change in length as the suspension moves. The outer joint has to allow suspension and steering movement up to about 45 degrees. A solid steel shaft transmits the drive.

Inner CV joint

Constant-Velocity Joint Operation

When a normal universal joint operates, the operating angle of the cross changes. This is what causes the speed variations. A constant-velocity joint spider (or cross) operates in one plane because the balls or rollers are free to move in slots. The cross bisects the driving and driven planes.

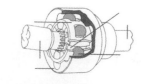

Details of a CV joint

Gaiter or Boot

The rubber boot or gaiter is used to keep out the dirt and water and to keep in the lubricant. Usually a graphite or molybdenum grease is used, but check the manufacturer's specifications to be sure.

Driveshaft gaiter

CV Joint Variations

There are a number of types of constant-velocity joints. The most common is the Rzeppa (pronounced reh-ZEP-ah). The inner joint must allow for axial movement due to changes in length as the suspension moves.

Suspension and steering movement

Rzeppa Joint

The Rzeppa joint is one of the most common. It has six steel balls held in a cage between an inner and outer race inside the joint housing. Each ball rides in its own track on the inner and outer races. The tracks are manufactured into an arch shape so that the balls stay in the midpoint at all times, ensuring that the angle of the drive is bisected. This joint is used on the outer end of a driveshaft. It will handle steering angles of up to 45 degrees.

CV joint – Rzeppa type

Cross-Groove Joint

The cross-groove constant-velocity joint is like a compact version of the Rzeppa joint. However, unlike the Rzeppa joint, the cross-groove type can plunge up to about 52 mm (2 inches). It is more compact, but the operating angle is limited to about 22 degrees. It can be used where space is a problem.

CV joint – Cross-groove type

Double-Offset Joint

The double-offset joint is a further variation of the Rzeppa joint. The main difference is that the outer race has long straight tracks. This allows a plunge (axial movement) of up to 55 mm (2.1 inches) and a steering angle of up to 24 degrees.

CV joint – Double-offset type

Tripod Joint

The tripod joint is different from other constant-velocity joints. A component called a spider splits the drive angle. The arms of the spider give it the tripod name. Each arm of the spider has needle roller bearings and a roller ball. The roller balls work in grooves in the housing. This joint is suitable for inner or outer positions.

CV joint – Tripod type

Summary

Driveshafts with constant-velocity joints are used on front-wheel drive vehicles. They transmit drive from the differential to each front wheel. They must also allow for suspension and steering movements. Inner joints must 'plunge' to allow for changes in length of the shaft. Several types of constant-velocity joints are used. All types work on the principle of bisecting the drive angle to produce a constant-velocity output.

A driveshaft transfers drive to the front wheels[2]

Read the last few pages again and note down FIVE bullet points here:

KC   Explain the purpose of a plunge type CV joint.

Types of Bearing

There are two main types of bearings used in rear-wheel hubs. These are ball bearings and roller (or tapered roller) bearings.

Notes

Ball bearing   Roller bearing

Rear-Wheel Bearings

Axle shafts transmit drive from the differential to the rear-wheel hubs. An axle shaft has to withstand:

Torsional stress due to driving and braking forces

Shear and bending stress due to the weight of the vehicle

Tensile and compressive stress due to turning forces

A number of bearing layouts are used – depending on the application – to handle these stresses.

Rough ground makes the stress on axle shafts even greater

Semi-Floating

Shown here is a typical axle mounting used on many rear-wheel drive cars. A single bearing is used, which is mounted in the axle casing. With this design, the axle shaft has to withstand all of the operating forces. The shaft is therefore strengthened and designed to do this. An oil seal is incorporated because oil from the final drive can work its way along the shaft. The seal prevents the brakes from being contaminated.

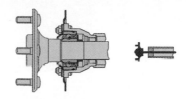

Wheel bearing – Semi-floating

Three-Quarter Floating

The three-quarter floating bearing shown here reduces the main shear stresses on the axle shaft, but the other stresses remain. The bearing is mounted on the outside of the axle tube. An oil seal is included to prevent the brake linings from being contaminated.

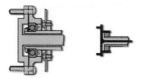

Wheel bearing – Three-quarter floating

Read the last few pages again and note down FIVE bullet points here:

Fully Floating

Fully floating systems are generally used on heavy, or off-road vehicles. This is because the stresses on these applications are greater. Two widely spaced bearings are used, which take all of the loads, other than torque, off the axle shaft. Bolts or studs are used to connect the shaft to the wheel hub. When these are removed, the shaft can be taken out without jacking up the vehicle.

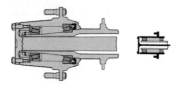

Wheel bearing – Fully floating

Front-Wheel Bearings

Front hubs on rear-wheel drive cars consist of two bearings. These are either ball or tapered roller types. The roller types are generally used on earlier vehicles. They have to be adjusted by tightening the hub nut and then backing it off by about half a turn. The more modern hub bearings, known as contact-type ball races, do not need adjusting. This is because the hub nut tightens against a rigid spacer. This nut must always be set at a torque specified by the manufacturer.

Front hub with tapered roller bearings

Front hub with ball bearings

Summary

The most common systems for rear-wheel drive cars are semi-floating rear bearings at the rear, and twin ball bearings at the front. The front bearings are designed to withstand side forces as well as vertical loads.

Rear hub

Front hub

KC   State the two main types of bearing used in rear-wheel hubs.

Introduction

Wheel bearings must allow smooth rotation of the wheels but also be able to withstand high stresses such as those generated when turning. Front-wheel drive arrangements must also allow the drive to be transmitted via the driveshafts.

Driveshaft and front hub

Notes

Front Bearings

The front hub works as an attachment for the suspension and steering as well as for supporting the bearings. It supports the weight of the vehicle at the front, when still or moving. Ball or roller bearings are used for most vehicles with specially shaped tracks. This is so that the bearings can withstand side loads when turning. The bearings support the driveshaft as well as the hub.

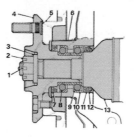

Front hub and bearings

Rear Bearings

The stub axle, which is solid-mounted to the suspension arm, fits in the center of two bearings. The axle supports the weight of the vehicle at the rear, when still or moving. Ball bearings are used for most vehicles with specially shaped tracks for the balls. This is so that the bearings can stand side loads when turning. A spacer is used to ensure the correct distance between, and pressure on the two bearings.

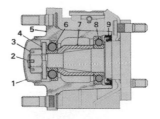

Rear hub and bearings

Summary

The hub and bearing arrangement on the front of a front-wheel drive car must bear weight, withstand driving forces, and support the driveshaft. The rear hub and bearings must support the vehicle and withstand side forces.

Rear hub   Front hub

Read the last few pages again and note down FIVE bullet points here:

KC   Describe the function of the front -wheel hub

Introduction

Four-wheel drive (4-WD) systems can be described as part-time or full-time. Part-time means that the driver has the choice of selecting the drive. All 4-wheel drive systems must include some type of transfer gearbox.

Four-wheel drive may be essential for this car![2]

Notes

Four-Wheel Drive System Layout

The main components of a four-wheel drive system are shown here. Each axle must be fitted with a differential. A transfer box takes drive from the output of the normal gearbox and distributes it to the front and rear. The transfer box may also include gears to allow the selection of a low ratio. High ratio is a straight-through drive.

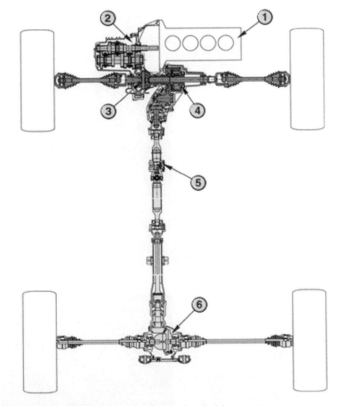

The main components of a four-wheel drive system[1]

Part-Time 4-Wheel Drive

A 4-wheel drive system, when described as part-time, means that the driver selects 4-wheel drive only when the vehicle needs more traction. When the need no longer exists, the driver reverts to the normal 2-wheel drive. This keeps driveline friction, and therefore the wear rate, to a minimum.

Selection control

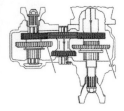

Transfer box - Neutral[1]

Full-Time 4-Wheel Drive

A 4-WD system, when described as full-time, means that the drive is engaged all the time. The driver may still be able to select a low-range setting. To prevent 'wind-up,' which would occur when the front and rear axles rotate at different speeds, a center differential or viscous drive is used.

Four-wheel drive in action (part-time)

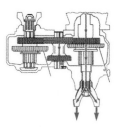

Transfer box – Two-wheel drive high[1]

All-Wheel Drive (A-WD)

An all-wheel drive system automatically transfers drive to the axle with better traction. It is designed for normal road use. A low-ratio option is not available. The system is described as part-time if the driver can select front-, or all-wheel drive. It is described as full-time if selection is not possible. The drive, on full-time systems, is passed to the rear via a viscous coupling. When the front wheels spin, the viscous coupling locks and transfers drive to the rear.

Volvo S60 AWD vehicle[2]

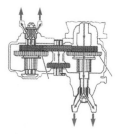

Transfer box – Four-wheel drive high[1]

Transfer Box

The transfer box of a part-time 4-WD system usually allows the driver to choose from four options: Neutral, 2-WD High, 4-WD High, and 4-WD Low. A typical system will have the transfer box, attached to the normal rear-wheel drive gearbox, in place of the extension housing. A two-speed transfer box is shown here.

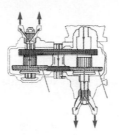

Transfer box – Four-wheel drive low[1]

Center Differential

A differential allows its two outputs to be driven at different speeds. This is normally important for the drive axle of a vehicle. When a vehicle is turning, the outer wheels travel faster than the inner wheels. On 4-WD systems, it is possible for, say, the front axle to rotate faster than the rear axle. This could produce driveline 'wind-up' of the transmission. Center differentials are designed to allow for this. On modern vehicles, these often consist of planetary-type gears.

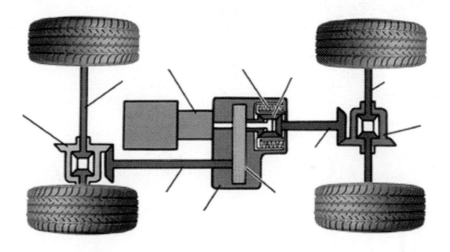

Differential fitted between front and rear axles

Viscous Coupling

A viscous coupling is designed to transmit drive when the axle speeds differ. This occurs because the difference in speed of the two axles increases the friction in the coupling. This results in greater torque transmission, which in turn reduces the speed difference. As the speed difference reduces, less torque is transmitted. In this way, the torque is shared proportionally between the two axles.

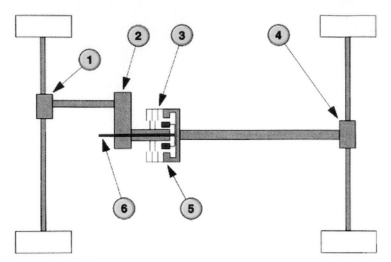

Torque is transmitted when axle speeds differ[1]

Chain Drive

A 'silent' drive chain is used on many newer vehicles to pass the drive to the auxiliary output shaft. The chain takes up less space than gears. It is designed to last the life of the vehicle and adjustment is not normally possible. The steel chain is similar in design to timing gear chains, except that it is wider and stronger.

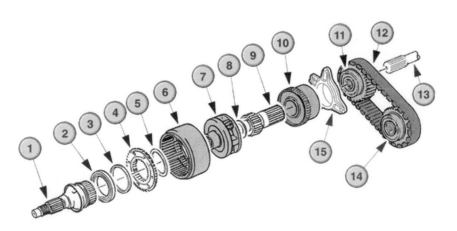

Transfer box using planetary gears and a drive chain[1]

Summary

Four-wheel drive systems use a combination of propshafts and driveshafts together with viscous couplings and transfer boxes. A number of variations are possible. These are described as full-time or part-time.

Read the last few pages again and note down FIVE bullet points here:

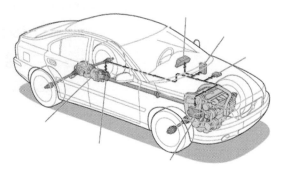

Volvo 4wd layout[2]

KC   State the FOUR usual settings/options of a transfer box selectable by the driver.

Module 3. Maintenance Operations
Section 1. Health and Safety

Notes

Safety First

Before carrying out any service or repair work, refer to all appropriate health and safety guidelines. Always follow all safety procedures and observe safety precautions when working on vehicles. Some specific hazards are listed in this section. General safety advice is also included.

Be smart, be safe[2]

Asbestos

Many types of brake-lining material and friction discs contain asbestos fibers. Always follow safety precautions when handling asbestos.

Breathing mask in use

Running Engines

Running engines are sometimes needed for diagnostics and system checks. A running engine presents two hazards: The first is the risk from rotating components and the second from the accumulation of exhaust gas in the workshop. Remain aware of rotating parts such as the fan, belt, and pulleys in the areas where you are likely to be working.

Be aware of moving parts

Electrically Driven Fans

An electrically driven fan is switched on automatically when the temperature of the coolant in the radiator rises above the switch operating temperature. This can occur even when the ignition is switched off. Always keep fingers out of the fan cowl and always remove the battery ground cable when the engine does not need to be running for diagnostic tests.

Fans can start at any time

Exhaust Emissions

When running an engine, it is important to prevent the build-up of exhaust gas in the workshop. Use extraction equipment or provide good ventilation.

Extraction equipment

Hot Compon- ents

When used for prolonged periods, vehicle components can become very hot. In particular, be careful not to touch the exhaust when working under the vehicle or on the engine.

Be aware of hot exhausts

Protective Clothing

Ideally, coveralls should be worn at all times. This protects your clothes as well as your skin. Gloves, goggles, breathing masks, hats, and strong footwear may also be necessary.

Personal protective equipment in use

Working Under Vehicles

There are a number of hazards to avoid when working below vehicles. One is the risk of hitting your head, which can obviously cause injury. Another risk is the possibility of getting rust and dirt in the eyes. Avoid these problems by wearing a bump cap and goggles whenever working under vehicles. The vehicle must always be supported safely before working underneath or alongside it.

Car on a ramp

Heavy Loads

The lifting and moving of heavy loads poses a risk. Many vehicle components fall into this category. Always tackle these tasks in an appropriate manner by being sure to use the recommended lifting equipment. Ask for assistance if necessary. Even some propshafts can be difficult to handle.

Even a propshaft can be heavy

Jacking and Supporting

Only use the recommended jacking and support points when lifting a vehicle. Refer to the manufacturer's instructions if unsure. Ensure that the jack and support stands, which must be used at all times, have an appropriate safe working load (SWL).

Jacking points

Skin Contact

When servicing vehicle systems avoid skin contact with new and used engine oils. Use barrier cream or non-porous gloves. Be careful with hot oil, particularly when carrying out oil-draining operations. Never keep oily rags in your coveralls or other pockets and change out of oil-contaminated clothing as soon as is reasonably possible.

Wear gloves or use barrier cream

Caution- Attention- Achtung!

All types of fuel (and particularly the vapors) are highly flammable. They can be ignited from a number of sources. Any exposed flame, a short circuit, a cigarette, or, under the right conditions, even a hot object will start a fire.

Take care!

Electrical Sparks

The most common cause of vehicle fires in the workshop is from electrical sparks. These can occur during the connection and removal of electrical terminals. Sparks also occur when the engine is cranked with the ignition on and the spark plugs removed. Disconnect the coil or connect the HT cables directly to ground to prevent this.

Sparks from the battery lead

Read the last few pages again and note down FIVE bullet points here:

Short Circuits

If a wire or tool is allowed to join the battery's positive connection to the negative connection, a serious short circuit will result. A wire would become extremely hot and, in addition to the obvious fire risk, would burn through whatever part of your body was touching it. The demonstration shown here was carried out by fully trained experts. Do NOT attempt to copy it. The same results occur if shorts are made on the vehicle. Be careful.

Do NOT try this!

Original Equipment

In consideration of other people's property, always be careful to use approved parts. Original equipment manufacturer's (OEM) parts may be required to meet safety regulations.

Use good quality parts

Refrigerant

Refrigerant used in air conditioning systems is dangerous. If it comes in contact with the skin, it produces severe frostbite. Wear protective goggles and gloves at all times. Use gloves designed for the purpose; leather or fabric gloves are NOT suitable. If refrigerant is exposed to exposed flames or hot surfaces, it produces toxic gases. Always ensure adequate ventilation when working on air-conditioning systems.

Air conditioning unit and equipment

Pressurized Cooling Systems

If work has to be done on the vehicle heater or the cooling system, there is a risk of scalding. The coolant is run at a pressure higher than atmospheric. If the cap is removed when hot, the coolant can boil instantly, spewing boiling water and steam.

Header tank

Rotating Driveline Components

The Ferrari shown here was tested on a rolling road. It was being driven at well in excess of 100 mph! Note how important it is to ensure that all driveline components are in good order.

Ferrari under test on a rolling road

Scheduled Servicing

Scheduled service requirements are often quite simple but important. Systems should be checked for correct operation. Adjustments, repairs, or replacements are then made if required. The particular servicing requirements for driveshafts are limited but nonetheless essential.

Notes

All systems need some maintenance[1]

Non-Routine Work

When carrying out routine maintenance, some non-routine work may be found. This should be reported to the driver or owner of the vehicle before expensive repairs are carried out.

Damaged CV gaiter

Workshop Tasks

Worksheets for routine maintenance of the system are included in this program. Refer to the safety precautions in the Health and Safety sections before carrying out any practical work on vehicles. The worksheets can be printed and used as part of a practical training program. They give general instructions only. Therefore, they should be used along with a manufacturer's workshop manual. Other good sources of information will also be required.

Refer to other sources of data as necessary

Worksheet

Service rear-wheel drive propshaft.

This task would normally be carried out as part of a general vehicle service and inspection. However, it may be necessary to check the propshaft at other times. Apply the parking brake and raise the vehicle on a hoist. Make sure the area is well lit so that you can see details. Exercise caution if the exhaust is still hot.

Propshaft

Propshaft

The first task is to check the propshaft for security and signs of damage. Make sure that any balance weights are secure. Look at the gearbox output seal where the propshaft sliding joint fits, and make sure it is not leaking. If the general area under the vehicle is oily, it may be necessary to steam clean it first.

Checking the universal joints

Universal Joints

Check all of the universal joints (UJs) for signs of leakage. If grease is leaking, this may be a sign that the universal joint is overheating and in need of replacement. Some types have a grease-point fitted. If this is the case, use a grease gun to pump new grease into each. Clean off any excessive grease. Finally, check all mounting bolts for security.

Grease gun[5]

Worksheet

Service front-wheel drive driveshafts.

This task would normally be carried out as part of a general vehicle service and inspection. However, it may be necessary to check the driveshafts at other times. Apply the handbrake and raise the vehicle on a hoist. Make sure the area is well lit so that you can see details. It is particularly important to check the area around the gaiters.

Driveshaft

Driveshafts

The first task is to check driveshafts for security and signs of damage. Make sure that any balance weights and dampers are secure. The dampers are simple rubber components, if fitted. Check for oil leaks from the final-drive output seals. Clean the area first and then check for clean oil. It may be necessary to take the vehicle on a road test in order to detect problems.

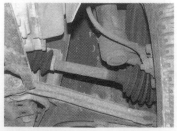

Driveshaft and CV gaiters in position

Constant-Velocity Joints

Be sure to check the constant-velocity joint gaiters/boots for signs of leakage. Look for signs of black grease. It is possible for the strap or cable tie that holds the gaiter to come loose. Replace gaiters if cuts or any other damage is evident. If grease has been lost, repack the joint with the correct type. Clean off any excess from the driveshaft and surrounding area. Finally, check the main driveshaft nut and any other flange bolts for security.

Checking the gaiters

Read the last few pages again and note down FIVE bullet points here:

Summary

The safety of all road users and pedestrians is essential. Reliable operation of the vehicle is also important. The condition of all systems is therefore vital. Carry out a check at all service intervals.

Safety is important[2]

Regular Checks

Regular servicing is vital for a customer's safety. Carry out checks at all services and report your findings to the customer. Advise customers if anything will need attention before the next scheduled service interval.

Explain any unusual conditions to the customer

Vehicle Condition

Respect your customer's vehicle and take precautions to keep it clean. Repairing or checking some systems is likely to involve you working under the vehicle and then sitting in the driver's seat. Use seat covers and ensure that the steering wheel is clean when you have finished.

Seat covers in use

Describing Noise

Driveline problems often result in unusual noises from the vehicle as it is used. Noise is very difficult to describe! However, the following screen describes some useful terms. These may be useful when discussing problems with your colleagues or customers.

Listening for noise

Noises

'Howling' or 'whining' tend to be noises associated with gears. Such sounds can occur at various speeds and driving conditions or they may be continuous. "Chuckle" is a rattling noise that sounds like a stick held against the spokes of a spinning bicycle wheel. It usually occurs while decelerating. "Knock" is very similar to "chuckle" though it may be louder and occurs during acceleration or deceleration.

A road test with the customer

Causes of Noise

Clicking, popping, or grinding noises may be noticeable at low speeds and be caused by:

Inner or outer constant-velocity joints worn (often due to lack of lubrication, so check for split gaiters)

Loose driveshaft

Another component coming in contact with a drive shaft

Damaged or incorrectly installed wheel bearing, brake, or suspension components.

Showing a customer the CV gaiter

Read the last few pages again and note down FIVE bullet points here:

Vibration

The following problems may cause vibration at normal road speeds:

Out-of-balance wheels

Out-of-round or damaged tires

The following may cause shudder or vibration during acceleration:

Damaged powertrain/drivetrain mounts

Excessively worn or damaged outboard or inboard constant-velocity joints

Damaged tire

Summary

A customer who is kept informed and treated with respect will return and keep you in a job! Explain things to customers when asked. Such courtesy will be appreciated.

Customers will return if they get good service

Module 4. Checking System Performance
Section 1. Checking the System

Introduction

System performance checks are routine activities that occur during all servicing work. They start at pre-delivery and continue for all scheduled service intervals.

Systems need checking regularly[2]

Quick Checks

Quick checks must be thorough because they are looking for incorrect operation or adjustment and the first signs of deterioration. Detailed diagnostic procedures may be required to identify faulty components. Always refer to manufacturer's data when necessary.

Manufacturer's data

Workshop Tasks

Worksheets for checking the performance of the system are included in this program. Refer to the safety precautions in the Health and Safety sections before carrying out any practical work on vehicles. The worksheets can be printed and used as part of a practical training program. They give general instructions only and should be used together with a manufacturer's workshop manual or other good sources of information.

Refer to other sources of data as necessary

Worksheet

Check driveline components.

The next few screens consider the propshaft used for rear-wheel drive and 4-wheel drive systems. First, select neutral and raise the vehicle on a hoist. Check for oil leaks from the propshaft sliding-joint at the gearbox output and from the differential/final drive input. Also, check for leaks from the universal joints.

Drive system layout[2]

Propshaft

To check the propshaft, start by holding one part of each universal joint in turn and trying to rotate the other part back and forth. Using a wrench, check the security of all fixing bolts. There are usually four at each end. Make sure that any balance weights on the shaft are secure. If a center bearing is fitted, check the bearing by rotating the propshaft (free the wheels for this). Make sure the mountings are secure and that the rubber is in good condition. If a donut drive is fitted, check it for security and condition.

Rear driveshaft or propshaft

Driveshafts

The next few screens consider the driveshafts used for front-wheel and 4-wheel drive systems. First, check for leaks from the differential output seals. Watch for leaks from the driveshaft boots/gaiters. Make sure the clips that hold them in place are secure. Check the security of any fixing nuts and bolts. Bolts are used to secure the inner part of some driveshafts to a drive flange.

CV joint gaiter

Driveshaft Movement

The driveshaft should have some axial movement (back and forth lengthways). However, there should be no rotational freeplay in the constant-velocity joints. Check this by holding each side of the joints and twisting. Check that any balance weights on the shaft are secure. If fitted, check that the damper is secure. The driveshaft main nut should be secure and be locked in place. This is usually done by a split pin or lock tab.

Driveshaft main nut

Worksheet

Checking for noise, vibration, and harshness (NVH).

To check for noise, vibration, and harshness, carry out a thorough visual inspection of the vehicle before conducting a road test. Look for leaks and loose nuts or bolts. Also, check for bright spots on drive shafts, which may indicate components rubbing. Check the tire pressures. Establish a drive test route that will be used for all diagnostic road tests. This allows you to get to know what is normal and what is not.

Checking a driveshaft

Road Test

Note the following during the road test. Use normal driving speeds of 20 to 80 km/h (15 to 50 mph):

Slowly accelerate and decelerate, listening for knocking.

At high speed, a vibration may be felt in the front floor pan or seats with no visible shake.

A vibration may be felt whenever the engine reaches a particular speed. It may disappear when coasting in neutral. Operating the engine at the problem speed while the vehicle is stationary may duplicate the vibration.

Use a familiar route for a road test

Noise and Vibration

In particular, check for noise and vibration while turning. Listen for clicking, popping, or grinding noises. These may be due to:

Damaged constant-velocity joints
A loose front wheel
Another component coming in contact with the driveshaft
Worn, damaged, or incorrectly installed wheel bearings
Damaged powertrain or drivetrain mountings

Damaged wheel bearing

Transmission Problems

After the road test, raise and support the vehicle with all of the wheels running free. Explore the speed range of interest, using the road test checks as previously discussed. Carry out a coast down test (overrun) in neutral. If the vehicle is free of vibration when operating at a steady engine speed but behaves very differently in drive and coast, a transmission problem is likely.

Car with wheels free on a hoist

Read the last few pages again and note down FIVE bullet points here:

Duplicated Conditions

A test on the hoist may produce different vibrations and noises than a road test. It is usual to find a vibration on the hoist that was not noticed during the road test. If the condition found on the road can be duplicated on the lift, carrying out experiments on the lift may save a great deal of time. Check all of the engine and transmission mountings.

Checking engine mountings

Summary

Driveline components make a contribution toward safety of the vehicle. System performance checks are therefore important. Cars are used at high speed and sudden breakdowns can be dangerous. Therefore, the systems should function correctly at all times.

Busy traffic!

Introduction

Some special test equipment is used when working with driveline components. Remember, you should always refer to the manufacturer's specific instructions for the equipment you are using.

Refer to manufacturer's instructions

Dial-Test Gauge

A dial-test gauge or dial-test indicator (DTI) is a useful piece of measuring equipment. It is usually used in conjunction with a magnetic stand. As the needle is moved, the dial (via a series of accurate gears) indicates the distance traveled. The graduations are either hundredths of a millimeter or thousandths of an inch.

DTI and stand

Torque Wrench

A good torque wrench is an essential piece of equipment. Many types are available but all work on a similar principle. Most are set by adjusting a screwed cylinder, which forms part of the handle. An important point to remember is that, as with any measuring tool, regular calibration is essential to ensure that it remains accurate.

A torque wrench is a useful tool[5]

Angle Locator

This magnetic device is used to check that the angles of a propshaft are equal. This is important because it ensures that the changing velocity effects of the universal joints are canceled out. The angle locator attaches magnetically to the shaft. A dial is set to zero and then, when it is moved to a new location, the difference in angle is indicated.

This device checks propshaft angles[5]

Accuracy

To ensure that measuring equipment remains accurate, there are just two simple guidelines:

Take care of your equipment – test equipment thrown on the floor will not be accurate.

Ensure that instruments are calibrated regularly. This means checking them against other equipment known to be in good working order.

Torque wrench in use

Read the last few pages again and note down FIVE bullet points here:

Introduction

The secret with finding faults is to have a good knowledge of the system and to work in a logical way. Use manufacturer's data and recommended procedures. This section includes general faultfinding procedures.

Check data before starting work

Symptoms and Problems

Remember that a symptom is the observed result of a problem. The next few screens each state a common symptom and possible problems. It is important to note that problems in one system can produce symptoms that may appear to be caused by another. Note also that the stated symptoms and problems may vary across different systems.

Symptoms are the result of faults

Vibration

Possible problems that could produce this symptom are:

Incorrect alignment of propshaft joints
Worn universal or constant-velocity joints
Bent shaft
Driveshaft out of balance
Mountings worn

Propshaft center bearing mounting

Grease leaking

Possible problems that could produce this symptom are:

Gaiters split
Clips loose
Universal joints overheating

CV gaiter

Knocking noises

Possible problems that could produce this symptom are:

Dry universal or constant-velocity joints
Worn constant-velocity joints (gets worse on tight turns)

Universal joint

No Drive

Possible problems that could produce this symptom are:

Broken driveshaft or propshaft
A problem with the transfer box selector or gear
Splined joint rounded off

Splines on a driveshaft

Systematic Testing

Working through a logical and systematic procedure for testing a system is the only reliable way to diagnose a problem. Use these six stages of faultfinding as a guide.

Verify the fault
Collect further information
Evaluate the evidence
Carry out further tests in a logical sequence
Fix the problem
Check all systems

Stages of faultfinding

Faultfinding Procedure

As an example of how the stages are applied, assume the reported symptom is a rumbling noise. Carrying out the procedures outlined over the next five screens would be a recommended method.

Check the latest data

Verify the Problem

Road test the car, with the customer if possible, to check the symptoms. Remember, it is not that you don't believe customers. Rather, it is often difficult for them to describe symptoms without technical knowledge.

Road test

Collect Further Information

Be sure, during the road test, that you drive the car through a variety of conditions. For example, make sharp and long turns in both directions. Drive at low speeds and at high speeds. Also, talk to the customer; for example, ask if the noise started suddenly or gradually.

Talk to the customer if possible

Evaluate the Evidence

Remember at this point to stop and think! If the noise has developed slowly, it may suggest a component such as a wheel bearing is wearing out. If the noise is noticeable all the time but worse on turning, it may help you to decide which bearing is at fault. Note however, that noisy bearings sometimes run quietly when loaded on turns.

Stop and think!

Carry out Further Tests

Jack up the car and support it on stands or use a wheel-free hoist if available. Spin each wheel in turn and listen for noise. Rock the wheel in and out at the top to check for bearing movement. It may also be necessary to run the wheels.

Checking the bearing freeplay

Fix the Problem

Once the suspect bearing has been identified, it must be replaced. Follow manufacturer's instructions for this task. Make sure that the new parts are of good quality.

Damaged wheel bearing

Check all Systems

It is possible, when fixing one fault, to accidentally cause a new problem. It is also possible that another fault exists, and it may appear to the customer that you have caused it! For both of these reasons, check that ALL systems work correctly after any repairs have been carried out.

CV gaiter

Summary

Faultfinding work is rewarding – when you find the fault! Remember to always work in a logical way. The stages of faultfinding can be applied to all systems on the vehicle, complex or simple.

Job finished

Read the last few pages again and note down FIVE bullet points here:

Module 5. Component Inspection and Repair
Section 1. Tools and Equipment

Introduction

Components will usually be removed, inspected, and repaired or replaced when a defect has been diagnosed. Other components are replaced, or stripped and cleaned, at scheduled mileage or time intervals. Refer to the Routine Maintenance section for details.

Good tools and equipment are important

Recommended Procedures

The descriptions provided in this section deal with the components for individual replacement rather than as a part of other work. Always refer to a workshop manual before starting work. You will also need to look for the recommended procedure, special tools, materials, tightening sequences, and torque settings. Some general and specific tools and pieces of equipment are described here.

Refer to data as required

General Toolkit

General tools and equipment will be required for most tasks. As your career develops you will build a collection of tools and equipment. Take care of your tools and they will serve you well.

Snap-on tools

Torque Wrench

A good torque wrench is an essential piece of equipment. Many types are available but all work on a similar principle. Most are set by adjusting a screwed cylinder, which forms part of the handle. An important point to remember is that, as with any measuring tool, regular calibration is essential to ensure that it remains accurate.

A torque wrench is a useful tool[5]

Air Guns

The whole point of power tools is that they do the work so you don't have to! Most air guns have an aluminum housing. This material is lightweight but gives long life. Air guns produce a hammer action. Because of this, impact sockets should be used. Normal sockets can shatter under this load. It is important to remember that air tools need lubricating from time to time.

Wheel gun[5]

Jacks and Stands

Most jacks are simple hydraulic devices. Remember to make sure the safe working load (SWL) is not exceeded. Ensure that any faults with equipment such as this are reported immediately. Axle stands must always be placed under the vehicle supporting the weight – before work is carried out.

Always use stands after jacking a vehicle[5]

Ramps and Hoists

Many ramps are available ranging from large four-post wheel-free types to smaller single-post lifts. These large items should be inspected regularly to ensure that they are safe.

Four-post lift in use

Transmission Jack

If a complete gearbox has to be removed, it is likely to be heavy! A transmission jack has attachments that allow you to support the gearbox and lower it safely. The equipment is hydraulically operated just like an ordinary jack. Often, the height can be set by using a foot pedal, which leaves both hands free for positioning the unit.

This jack will support a gearbox[5]

Bearing Puller

Removing some bearings is difficult without a proper puller. For internal bearings, the tool has small legs and feet that hook under the bearing. A threaded section is tightened to pull out the bearing. External pullers hook over the outside of the bearing and a screwed thread is tightened against the shaft.

Internal and external bearing pullers[5]

Read the last few pages again and note down FIVE bullet points here:

Air Ratchet

These tools are very useful for removing or fitting nuts and bolts. However, it is possible to overtighten if care is not taken. Air tools can be very powerful and will trap your hands! Take adequate precautions at all times.

These tools are very useful[5]

Slide Hammer

A slide hammer is a form of puller. It consists of a steel rod over which a heavy mass slides. The mass is 'hammered' against a stop, thus applying a pulling action. The clamp end of the tool can screw either into, or onto, the component. Alternatively, puller legs with feet are used to grip under the sides of the component.

This tool is useful for removing halfshafts[5]

Grease Gun

A grease gun is a simple device that pumps grease under pressure. A special connector fits onto a grease nipple. Some types are air operated but the one shown here is a simple pump-action type.

Some older UJs can be lubricated[5]

Workshop Tasks

Worksheets for removing, replacing, stripping, and rebuilding the system are included in this program. Refer to the safety precautions in the Health and Safety sections before carrying out any practical work on vehicles. The worksheets can be printed and used as part of a practical training program. They give general instructions only and should therefore be used together with a manufacturer's workshop manual or some other good source of information.

Refer to other sources of data as necessary

Notes

Worksheet

Remove and refit wheel bearings.

Apply the parking brake and loosen the road wheel nuts. Raise the front or rear of the vehicle as required, support it on stands, and remove the road wheel. The methods outlined here are generic. Refer to manufacturer's data for specific instructions.

Wheel being removed for repair work

Front Hub Assembly

Remove the driveshaft nut split pin. Use an assistant to apply firm pressure to the brake pedal and, while the brake is applied, unscrew the driveshaft nut. Remove the brake caliper and the disc. Using a ball-joint breaker tool, disconnect the joint from the steering arm. Unscrew the nuts and remove the bolts to release the strut from the hub assembly. Unscrew the nut and remove the clamp bolt securing the lower ball joint to the hub assembly. Place a suitable lever between the lower arm and the anti-roll bar. Push downward to release the ball joint from the hub. Finally, remove the hub from the driveshaft.

Removing the hub nut

Bearings and Seals

Extract the inner oil seal, spacer, and outer oil seal. Drive out one of the bearings, invert the hub, and drive out the remaining bearing. Inspect the bearings for signs of wear and damage; replace as necessary. Pack the new bearings with suitable grease and press them into the hub. Fit the oil seals and spacer. Locate the hub on the driveshaft. Fit the flat washer and driveshaft nut.

Front hub components

Refitting the Hub

Fit the hub assembly to the lower ball joint, fit the clamp bolt, and tighten the nut. Fit the hub to the strut, fit the bolts, and tighten the nuts to the correct torque. Connect the ball joint to the steering lever and fit and tighten the nut. Fit the disc to the drive flange and tighten the securing screws. Fit the brake caliper. Use an assistant to apply firm pressure to the brake pedal and, while the brake is applied, tighten the driveshaft nut to the correct torque. Lock the nut with a new split pin. Fit the road wheel and nuts.

Lower ball joint

Rear Hub Assembly

Withdraw the grease retainer cap from the center of the hub and extract the split pin from the stub shaft. Unscrew the hub nut, remove the flat washer, and withdraw the hub and brake drum assembly. Extract the hub oil seal, drive the inner bearing out, and collect the spacer. Invert the hub and brake drum assembly and drive out the outer bearing. Inspect the bearings for signs of wear and damage; replace as necessary.

Rear hub components

Bearings

Pack the bearings with suitable grease and press the outer bearing into the hub with the side marked THRUST facing outward. Invert the hub, fit the spacer, and press the inner bearing with the side marked THRUST outward into the hub. Dip the new oil seal in oil and press it into the hub (sealing lip facing inward). Fit the hub and brake drum assembly to the stub shaft, fit the flat washer, and fit and tighten the hub nut to the cor-rect torque. Lock the nut with a new split pin. Fit the grease retainer cap, and then fit the road wheel and nuts.

Packing bearings with grease

Read the last few pages again and note down FIVE bullet points here:

Worksheet

Remove and refit driveshaft.

Apply the parking brake and loosen the road wheel nuts. Raise the front of the vehicle, support it on stands, and remove the road wheel. Remove the driveshaft nut split pin or lock tab. Use an assistant to apply the foot brake and then remove the driveshaft nut and washer.

Driveshaft

Driveshaft Removal

Split the steering track rod end from the steering arm and remove it. Remove the bolts securing the hub to the suspension strut. Pivot the hub outward to the limit of its movement, but be careful not to strain the brake hose. Maneuver the driveshaft from the hub. Carefully pry between the driveshaft inner joint and the differential housing to release the spring ring. Withdraw the driveshaft.

Splitting the track rod end joint

Driveshaft Refitting

To refit, slide the shaft into the differential housing until the spring ring engages. Maneuver the outer end of the driveshaft into the hub and fit the nut and washer. A new nut may be required by some manufacturers. Refit the suspension strut and the steering joint. Use an assistant to apply the foot brake and then tighten the driveshaft nut to the specified torque. Fit a new split pin or knock in the tab as required. Refit the road wheel and lower the vehicle. Torque the wheel nuts and road test.

Refitting the strut

Introduction

The main inspections and measurements carried on the system are included in this section. Inspections should take place at scheduled service intervals, and if problems have been reported.

Driveshaft

Workshop Tasks

Worksheets for inspections and measurement of the system are included in this section. Refer to the safety precautions in the Health and Safety sections before carrying out any practical work on vehicles. The worksheets can be printed and used as part of a practical training program. They give general instructions only. Therefore, they should be used along with a manufacturer's workshop manual, or some other good source of information.

Refer to data as required

Worksheet

Measure propshaft/driveshaft run-out.

Raise the vehicle on a hoist and free the driven wheels. Clean the three bands around the propshaft/driveshaft at the front, center, and rear. Mount a dial gauge on a magnetic stand and attach the stand to a solid part of the vehicle body.

Propshaft

Run Out Readings

Take run-out readings at the front, center, and rear of the shaft. If necessary, unbolt and disconnect the shaft at one end, turn it half a turn, and reconnect. Take run-out readings at the front, center, and rear of the propshaft/driveshaft once again. Compare readings to the manufacturer's specifications. If necessary, replace the propshaft/driveshaft.

Dial gauge in position

Worksheet

Strip down the CV joint and assess its condition. Remove the driveshaft from the vehicle as described in the appropriate worksheet. Release the two clips securing the outer joint gaiter/boot.

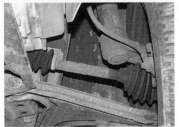
CV joint gaiter

Read the last few pages again and note down FIVE bullet points here:

CV Joint Removal

Peel back the boot to expose the joint and use a hide mallet to drive the joint from the shaft. Remove the spring ring from the shaft and remove the gaiter/boot. Examine the shaft, gaiters/boots, and joints for wear and damage. Replace as required. On many systems, the complete shaft must be replaced if the inner joint is damaged because it forms part of the main shaft.

Removing the CV joint

CV Joint Rebuild

To rebuild, fit the gaiter and a new spring ring. Compress the ring so that the outer joint can be fitted onto the shaft. Use a hide mallet to drift the joint into place over the spring ring. Pack the joints with grease as specified by the manufacturer and secure the gaiters. Refit the driveshaft to the vehicle as described in the appropriate worksheet.

Securing the gaiter

Summary

Some repairs require a lot of work. However, do not make any compromises. Keep your customers, and yourself, happy and safe.

Job finished!

TOPIC: FINAL DRIVE & DIFFERENTIAL

Module 1. Transmission Final Drive
Section 1. Introduction to Transmission

Introduction

Transmission is a general term used to describe all the components required to transmit power from the engine to the wheels. The requirement is to convert the power from the relatively high velocity and low torque of the engine crankshaft, to the variable, usually lower speed and higher torque needed at the wheels. This first section is a general introduction to the transmission system.

Transmission components are important[2]

Types of Transmission

The two basic types of transmission use either a manual gearbox, in which the gears are selected by the driver, or an automatic gearbox, in which the gears are changed automatically. The other driveline components, with the exception of the clutch, are the same for automatic and manual systems.

Manual transmission

Automatic transmission

Front-Wheel Drive Transmission

Working from the engine to the wheels, the main components of a typical front-wheel drive transmission system are as follows:

Clutch

Gearbox

Final drive

Differential

Driveshafts

Clutch   Gearbox   Final drive and   Driveshaft
                                 differential

Rear-Wheel Drive Transmission

Working from the engine to the wheels, the main components of a typical rear-wheel drive transmission system are as follows:

Clutch

Gearbox

Propshaft

Final drive

Differential

Halfshafts

Clutch   Gearbox[2]   Propshaft   Final drive and
                                                       differential

Clutch

Fitted between the engine and gearbox, the clutch allows the drive to be disconnected when the pedal is depressed. It allows a smooth take-up of drive and allows gears to be changed.

Clutch assembly

Manual Gearbox

A manual gearbox is a box full of gears of varying ratios. The gear ratio most suitable for the driving conditions is selected by the driver. Most boxes contain approximately thirteen gear cogs, which allow five forward gears and one reverse.

A box of gears!

Torque Converter

A torque converter is sometimes called a fluid flywheel (although the two differ slightly) and is used in conjunction with an automatic gearbox. It is in two main parts. As the input section rotates, fluid pressure begins to act on the output section, which is made to rotate. As speed increases, a better drive is made. The drive therefore takes up automatically and smoothly.

Details of a torque converter

Automatic Gearbox

As the name suggests, this is a gearbox which operates automatically. Most types contain special gear arrangements known as epicyclic gear trains. Some now use complicated electronic control, but the basic principle is that fluid pressure from a pump, which changes with road speed, is used to change the gears.

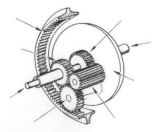

Epicyclic gears are often used in an 'auto-box'[1]

Final Drive

To produce the required torque at the road wheels, a fixed gear reduction from the high engine speed is required. The final drive consists of just two gears with a ratio of about 4:1. These are bevel gears on rear-wheel drive systems and normal gears on front-wheel drive.

Differential and final drive combination

Differential

A differential is a special combination of gears which allows the driven wheels of a vehicle to rotate at different speeds. Think of a car going around in a circle. The outer wheel has to travel a greater distance, and hence must rotate at a faster speed than the inner wheel. If the differential wasn't used, the drive would 'wind up' and something would break.

The differential can be called a torque equalizer

Driveshafts

Two driveshafts are used to pass the drive from the outputs of the final drive to each wheel. Each driveshaft contains two constant-velocity joints. These joints are covered with a rubber boot to keep out water and dirt.

This shaft transmits drive to the wheels

Propshaft

On rear-wheel drive vehicles, the drive has to be transferred from the gearbox output to the final drive and differential unit in the rear axle. The propshaft, short for propeller shaft, is a hollow tube with a universal joint at each end. If removed, the universal joints (UJs) must be aligned correctly.

This shaft transmits drive to the final drive

Universal Joint

A UJ is like a cross with a bearing on each leg. It allows drive to be transmitted through an angle. This allows for suspension movement.

This is called a UJ

Read the last few pages again and note down FIVE bullet points here:

Constant-Velocity Joint

The constant-velocity joint is similar to a UJ. It is used on front-wheel drive driveshafts. It allows a smooth, constant-velocity drive to be passed through, even when the suspension moves up and down and the steering moves side to side.

CV joints allow for this movement

Summary

Driveline components are key parts of the transmission system. However, they must work in conjunction with other parts. All should be operating correctly for optimum performance.

Driveshafts in use[2]

KC

Describe the construction AND purpose of a universal joint.

Introduction

Because of the speed at which an engine runs, and in order to produce enough torque at the road wheels, a fixed gear reduction is required. This is known as the final drive. It consists of just two gears. On front-wheel drive vehicles, the final drive is fitted after the output of the gearbox. On rear-wheel drive vehicles, it is fitted in the rear axle after the propshaft.

Front -wheel final drive

Rear-wheel final drive

Gear Ratio

The ratio is normally between 2:1 and 4:1. In other words, at 4:1, when the gearbox output is turning at 4000 rev/min, the wheels will turn at 1000 rev/min.

Gear train drive ratio

Rear-Wheel Drive

The final drive gears turn the drive through ninety degrees on rear-wheel drive vehicles. Four-wheel drive vehicles will also have this arrangement as part of the rear axle.

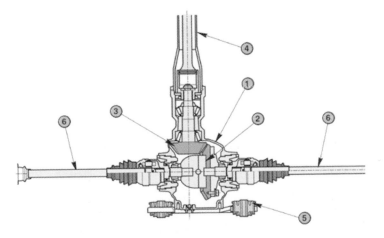
Rear axle final drive gears[1]

Front-Wheel Drive

Most cars now have a transverse engine, which drives the front wheels. The power of the engine, therefore, does not have to be carried through a right angle to the drive wheels. The final drive contains ordinary reducing gears rather than bevel gears.

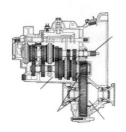

Transaxle final drive gears[1]

Bevel Gears

The crown wheel and pinion are types of bevel gears because they mesh at right angles to each other. They carry power through a right angle to the drive wheels. The crown wheel is driven by the pinion, which receives power from the propeller shaft.

Bevel gears change ratio and drive angle

Reduced Speed and Increased Torque

Final drive gears reduce the speed from the propeller shaft and increase the torque. The reduction in the final drive multiplies any reduction that has already taken place in the transmission.

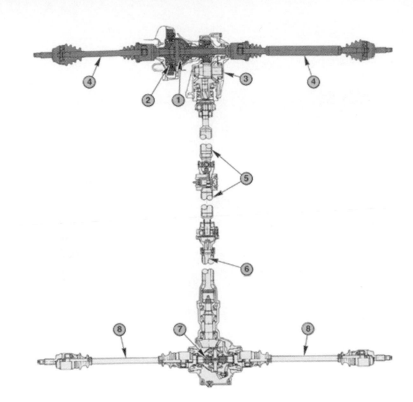

4WD final drive layout[1]

Hypoid Gear

The crown wheel gear of a rear-wheel drive system is usually a hypoid type, which is named after the way the teeth are cut. This results in quiet operation and allows the pinion to be set lower than the crown wheel center. This saves space in the vehicle because a smaller transmission tunnel can be used.

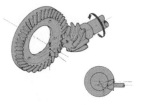

The design allows a lower propshaft to be used

Hypoid Gear Oil

Because the teeth of hypoid gears cause 'extreme pressure' on the lubrication oil, a special type of oil is used. This oil may be described as 'Hypoid Gear Oil' or 'EP', which stands for extreme pressure. As usual, refer to manufacturers' recommendations when topping off or changing oil.

Lubrication is important

Read the last few pages again and note down FIVE bullet points here:

Rear Axle

The complete rear axle assembly consists of other components as well as the final drive gears. The other main components are the differential, halfshafts, and bearings. Components that make up a solid axle are shown here. Some rear-wheel drive and four-wheel drive vehicles have a split axle. On these types, the final drive is mounted to the chassis, and driveshafts are used to connect to the wheels.

Rear axle components (click to zoom in/out)

Front Axle

The front-wheel drive axle, where a transaxle system is used, always consists of the final drive and two driveshafts. The gearbox, final drive, and one driveshaft are shown here. The final drive gears provide the same reduction as those used on rear, wheel drives, but do not need to turn the drive through ninety degrees.

Front-wheel drive components

Four-Wheel Drive

The general layout of a four-wheel drive system is shown here. A representation of how torque is distributed is also shown. The variation in torque is achieved by differential action. This is examined in more detail later in this program.

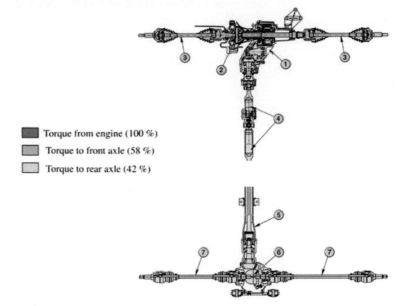

■ Torque from engine (100 %)
□ Torque to front axle (58 %)
□ Torque to rear axle (42 %)

Torque distribution in a 4WD system[1]

Summary

To produce enough torque at the road wheels, a fixed gear reduction is required. This is known as the final drive. It consists of just two gears. On rear-wheel drive systems, the gears are beveled to turn the drive through ninety degrees. On front-wheel drive systems, this is not necessary. The drive ratio is similar for front- and-rear-wheel drive cars.

Is this the final drive?[2]

KC   Describe the purpose of final drive gears.

Introduction

The 'steerability' of a vehicle is lost if the wheels spin during severe acceleration. Electronic traction control has been developed as a supplement to antilock brake systems (ABS). This control system prevents the wheels from spinning when moving off, or when accelerating sharply while on the move. In this way, an individual wheel, which is spinning, is braked in a controlled manner. If both or all of the wheels are spinning, the drive torque is reduced by means of an engine control function. Traction control has become known as ASR or TCR.

Notes

Traction control would have prevented this!

Antilock Brake System (ABS)

Traction control is normally available in combination with ABS. This is because many of the components required are the same for each. Shown here is a block diagram of a traction control system. Note the links with ABS and the engine control system.

Traction control system

Reasons for Traction Control

Traction control will intervene to achieve the following:

Driving stability

Reduction of yawing moment reactions

Optimum propulsion at all speeds

Reduced driver workload

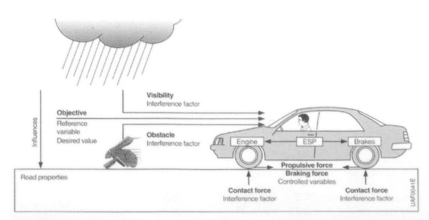

'Conditions' acting on the driver and car[3]

Intervention

An automatic control system can intervene more quickly and precisely than the driver of the vehicle. This allows stability to be maintained at a time when the driver might not be able to cope with the situation.

ABS and traction control modulator and ECU[4]

Control Methods

Control of tractive force can be achieved by a number of methods:

Throttle control

Ignition control

Braking effect

Each of these methods is examined further over the next three screens.

Throttle   Brakes   Ignition   System under test

Throttle Control

Throttle control can be through an actuator, which simply moves the throttle cable. If the vehicle employs a 'drive by wire' accelerator, then control will be in conjunction with the engine management system. This throttle control will be independent of the driver's pedal position. This method alone works, but it is relatively slow to control engine torque.

Wheel spin reduction using throttle control

Ignition Control

If ignition is retarded, the engine torque can be reduced up to 50% in a very short space of time. The timing is adjusted by a set ramp value from the actual ignition value.

Wheel spin reduction using throttle and ignition control

Braking Effect

If the spinning wheel is restricted by brake pressure, the reduction in torque at the affected wheel is very fast. Maximum brake pressure is not used in order to ensure that passenger comfort is maintained.

Wheel spin reduction using throttle and brake control

Traction Control System

A sensor determines the position of the accelerator and, taking into account other variables such as engine temperature and speed, the throttle is set at the optimum position by a drive motor. When accelerating, the increase in engine torque leads to an increase in driving torque at the wheels. In order for optimum acceleration, the maximum possible driving torque must be transferred to the road. If driving torque exceeds that which can be transferred, then wheel slip will occur.

Throttle actuator

Wheel Spin

When wheel spin is detected, the throttle position and ignition timing are adjusted. However, better results are gained when the brakes are applied to the spinning wheel. When the brakes are applied, a valve in the hydraulic modulator assembly moves over to allow traction control operation. This allows pressure from the pump to be applied to the brakes on the offending wheel. The valves, in the same way as for ABS, can provide pressure build-up, pressure hold, and pressure reduction. This all takes place without the driver touching the brake pedal.

Hydraulic modulator assembly

Read the last few pages again and note down FIVE bullet points here:

Electronic Stability Program (ESP)

ESP systems intervene to ensure stability under a wide range of situations. Shown here is the difference between a vehicle with and without a stability control system. Sensors supply an electronic control unit with information on vehicle movement, such as rotation about a vertical axis. This is known as yaw. By controlling the driving force from the engine and the braking force to individual wheels, the vehicle can be kept in a stable condition. This occurs even if the driver is not fully in control!

Results of ESP

Summary

Traction control is designed to prevent wheel spin when a vehicle is accelerating. This improves traction and ensures vehicle stability. Antilock brakes and traction control have now developed into complex stability control systems.

Bosch test car on the skid pan[4]

KC

Explain why traction control is not normally available as an independent system, but in combination with ABS.

State THREE methods of controlling tractive force used by traction control systems.

Module 2. Differentials
Section 1. Differential Operation

Introduction

The differential is a set of gears that divides the torque evenly between the two drive wheels. The differential allows one wheel to rotate faster than the other. As a car goes around a corner, the outside driven wheel travels further than the inside one. The outside wheel must therefore rotate faster than the inside one to cover the greater distance in the same time.

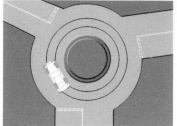

The outer wheels travel a greater distance

Main Components

The differential consists of sets of bevel gears and pinions within a cage, attached to the large final drive gear. The bevel gears can be described as sun and planet gears. The sun gears provide the drive to the wheels via halfshafts or driveshafts. The planet gears either rotate with the sun gears or rotate around them, depending on whether the car is cornering or not.

Final drive and differential components (click to zoom in/out)

Final Drive Gears

The small pinion brings the drive from the gearbox to the larger final drive gear. A fixed gear reduction is produced by the crown wheel and pinion. On rear-wheel drive cars, bevel gears are used to turn the drive through ninety degrees.

Final drive and differential (click to zoom in/out)

Differential Casing and Bearings

The bearings support the differential casing, which is bolted to the final drive gear. The casing transmits the drive from the final drive gear to the planet gear pinion shaft.

Final drive and differential (click to zoom in/out)

Sun and Planet Pinions

The planet gears are pushed around by their shaft. The sun gear pinions, which are splined to the drive shafts, take their drive from the planet gears. The sun gears always rotate at the same speed as the road wheels.

Planet Shaft

The planet shaft is secured in the differential casing so that it pushes the planet gears. If the sun gears, which are attached to the road wheels via the driveshafts, are moving at the same speed, the planet gears do not spin on their shaft. However, when the vehicle is cornering, the sun gears need to move at different speeds. In this case, the planet gears spin on the shaft to make up for the different wheel speeds.

Traveling In a Straight Line

When the vehicle is traveling in a straight line, the bevel pinions (planet gears) turn with the sun gears, but do not rotate on their shaft. This occurs because the two sun gears attached to the driveshafts are revolving at the same speed.

Planet gears rotate with the sun gears

Cornering

When the vehicle is cornering, the bevel pinions (planet gears) roll around the sun gears, and rotate on their shaft. This rotation is what allows the outer wheel to turn faster than the inner.

Planet gears rotate around the sun gears

Torque Equalizer

A standard differential can be described as a torque equalizer. This is because the same torque is provided to each wheel, even if they are revolving at different speeds. At greater speeds, more power is applied to the wheel, so the torque remains the same.

Differential

Read the last few pages again and note down FIVE bullet points here:

Extreme Example

One further way to understand the differential action is to consider the extreme situation. This is when the corner is so sharp, the inner wheel does not move at all! Now of course this is impossible, but it can be simulated by jacking up one wheel of the car. All the drive is transferred to the free wheel. The planets roll around the stationary sun wheel but drive the free wheel because they are rotating on their shaft.

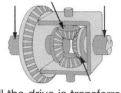

All the drive is transferred to the free wheel

Read the last few pages again and note down FIVE bullet points here:

Stuck In The Mud!

The example, given on the last screen, highlights the one problem with a differential. If one of the driven wheels is stuck in the mud, all the drive is transferred to that wheel and it normally spins. Of course, in this case, drive to the wheel on the hard ground would be more useful. The solution to this problem is the limited slip differential.

No drive goes to the wheel on the ground

Summary

As a car goes around a bend, the outside driven wheel travels further than the inside one. The outside wheel must therefore rotate faster to cover the greater distance in the same time. The differential allows this difference in speed.

The handling would be very poor without a differential[4]

KC

State the purpose of a differential.

Describe what happens to the planet gears when a vehicle is driven with one wheel spinning in mud.

Introduction

Some higher performance vehicles use a limited slip differential (LSD). Clutch plates, or similar, are connected to the two output shafts and can control the amount of slip. This can be used to counteract the effect of one wheel losing traction when high power is applied.

High-performance vehicles use LSDs[2]

Standard Differential

A standard differential always applies the same amount of torque to each wheel. Two factors determine how much torque can be applied to a wheel. In dry conditions, when there is plenty of traction, the amount of torque applied to the wheels is limited by the engine and gearing. When the conditions are slippery, such as on ice, the torque is limited by the available grip.

This differential is sometimes described as an open type

Limited Slip Differential

The solution to the problems of the normal differential is the limited slip differential (LSD). Limited slip differentials use various mechanisms to allow normal differential action when going around turns. However, when a wheel slips, they allow more torque to be transferred to the non-slipping wheel.

LSD in position[2]

The Clutch-Type LSD

The clutch-type LSD is the most common. It is the same as a standard differential, except that it also has a spring pack and a multi-plate clutch. The spring pack pushes the sun gears against the clutch plates, which are attached to the cage. Both sun gears spin with the cage when both wheels are moving at the same speed, and the clutches have little or no effect. However, the clutch plates try to prevent either wheel from spinning faster than the other. The stiffness of the springs and the friction of the clutch plates determine how much torque it takes to make it slip.

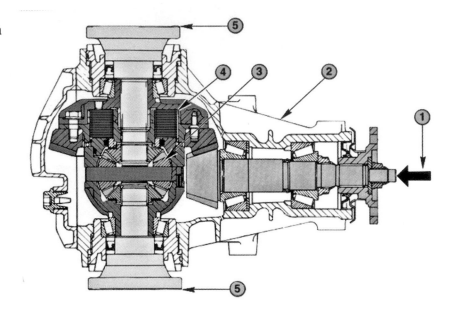

LSD using clutch plates[1]

Slippery Surface

If one drive wheel is on a slippery surface and the other one has good traction, drive can be transmitted to this wheel. The torque supplied to the wheel not on the slippery surface is equal to the amount of torque it takes to overpower the clutches. The result is that the car will move, but not with all the available power.

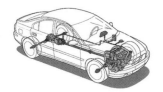

4x4 layout using LSDs[2]

Viscous Coupling

The viscous coupling is often found in all-wheel-drive vehicles. It is commonly used to link the back wheels to the front wheels so that when one set of wheels starts to slip, torque will be transferred to the other set. The viscous coupling has two sets of plates inside a sealed housing that is filled with a thick fluid. One set of plates is connected to each output shaft. Under normal conditions, both sets of plates and the viscous fluid spin at the same speed. However, when one set of wheels spins faster, there will be a difference in speed between the two sets of plates.

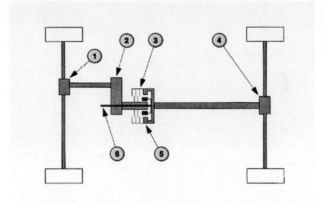

Viscous effect of an egg!

Viscous type LSD

Viscous Fluid

The viscous fluid between the plates tries to catch up with the faster disks, dragging the slower disks along. This transfers more torque to the slower wheels. When a vehicle is cornering, the difference in speed between the wheels is not as large as when one wheel is slipping. The faster the plates spin relative to each other, the more torque the coupling transfers. This effect can be demonstrated by spinning an egg. Spin the egg and then stop it. Let go, and it will start to spin again as the viscous fluid inside is still spinning and drags the shell around with it.

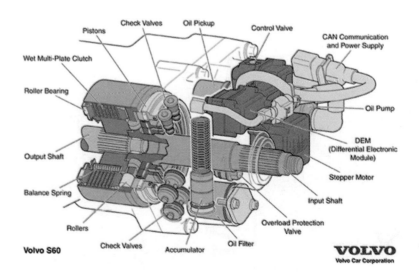

Electronically controlled coupling[2]

Electronic Control

Conventional limited slip differentials cannot be designed for optimum performance because of the effect on the vehicle when cornering and on the steering. These issues prompted the development of electronic control. The slip limiting action is controlled by a multi-disc clutch as discussed previously. The pressure on the clutch plates is controlled by hydraulic pressure, which in turn is controlled by a solenoid valve under the influence of an ECU. If required it can fully lock the axle. Data is provided to the ECU from standard ABS type wheel sensors.

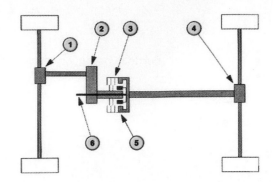

Electronic control of drive system[2]

Summary

The two main types of limited slip differentials are the plate type and viscous coupling type. A speed difference between wheels or axles must overcome plate friction on the clutch type. The viscous type works because the friction between plates increases as the speed difference increases.

Rally cars use LSDs[2]

Read the last few pages again and note down FIVE bullet points here:

KC   Describe the basic operation of a limited slip differential.

Introduction

Some differentials are provided with a facility that locks them. In other words, they stop being differentials! This is useful for some off-road situations. Disconnect units are now also being used to improve overall performance of AWD systems.

Off-road vehicle

Differential Locks

Differential locks are used on many off-road type vehicles. A simple dog clutch or similar device prevents the differential action. This allows far better traction on slippery surfaces. An electric, hydraulic, or pneumatic mechanism is used to lock the two output pinions together.

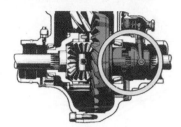

Locking mechanism

Diff Lock Control

This mechanism is usually activated manually by switch, and, when activated, both wheels will spin at the same speed. If one wheel ends up off the ground, the other wheel will continue to spin at the same speed.

Diff lock warning light

4x4 Power Flow

Many 4x4 vehicles use three differentials, one on each axle and one joining the two axles. For optimum handling, it is essential to control the torque distribution. Shown here is a typical system with the torque distribution and main components highlighted.

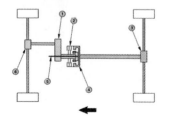

Power flow with a 4WD configuration[1]

Disconnect Unit - Purpose

This type of unit provides ABS compatibility for AWD. It can provide AWD function in reverse by automatic actuation of a centrifugal locking mechanism. It is a simple, self-controlled system, requiring no external control. The disconnect unit (DU) is an automatically locking freewheel device. It utilizes a viscous transmission or similar system as a hang-on (also known as 'on-demand') driveline configuration.

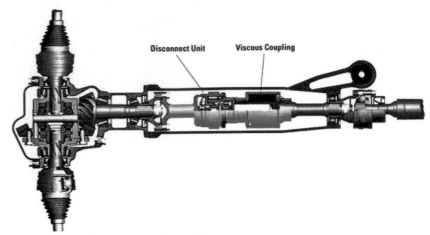

DU positioned in the transmission ^{ZF}

Disconnect Unit - Operation

The unit transmits torque in the forward drive direction. However, in the overrun mode, when braking, the unit allows no torque transmission between the front and rear axles. This feature provides optimum vehicle braking stability. An integrated coupling bypasses the overrun mode by locking the unit at lower speeds. This provides AWD capability in reverse drive. When the predefined disengagement speed is exceeded, flyweights open the coupling and the overrun feature is restored.

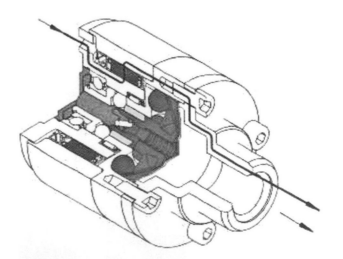

DU freewheel components ^{ZF}

Read the last few pages again and note down FIVE bullet points here:

Summary

There are a number of new features under development relating to differentials. Locking units are often used on off-road vehicles. Disconnect units allow improved drive performance but without loss of vehicle control.

Off-road vehicle in action[2]

KC   State the benefit of a disconnect unit.

Module 3. Maintenance Operations
Section 1. Health and Safety

Safety First

Before carrying out any service or repair work, refer to all appropriate health and safety guidelines. Always follow all safety procedures and observe safety precautions when working on vehicles. Some specific hazards are listed in this section. General safety advice is also included.

Be smart, be safe[2]

Asbestos

Many types of brake lining material and friction discs contain asbestos fibers. Always follow safety precautions when handling asbestos.

Breathing mask in use

Running Engines

Running engines are sometimes needed for diagnostics and system checks. A running engine presents two hazards; the first is the risk from rotating components and the second from the accumulation of exhaust gas in the workshop. Remain aware of rotating parts such as the fan, belt, and pulleys in the areas where you are likely to be working.

Be aware of moving parts

Electrically Driven Fans

An electrically driven fan is switched on automatically, when the temperature of the coolant in the radiator rises above the switch operating temperature. This can occur even when the ignition is switched off. Always keep fingers out of the fan cowl and always remove the battery ground lead, when the engine does not need to be running, for diagnostic tests.

Fans can start at any time

Exhaust Emissions

When running an engine, it is important to prevent the build-up of exhaust gas in the workshop. Use extraction equipment or provide good ventilation.

Extraction equipment

Hot Components

When used for prolonged periods, vehicle components can become very hot. In particular, take care not to touch the exhaust when working under the vehicle or on the engine.

Be aware of hot exhausts

Protective Clothing

Overalls should ideally be worn at all times. This protects your clothes as well as your skin. Gloves, goggles, breathing masks, hats, and strong footwear may also be necessary. Refer to local regulations for any special requirements.

Personal protective equipment in use

Working below Vehicles

There are a number of hazards to avoid when working below vehicles. One is the risk of hitting your head, which can obviously cause injury. Another risk is the possibility of getting rust and dirt in the eyes. Avoid these problems by wearing a cap and goggles whenever working below vehicles. The vehicle must always be supported safely before working underneath or alongside it.

Car on a ramp

Heavy Loads

A risk is present if a task requires the lifting and moving of heavy loads. Many vehicle components fall into this category. Always tackle these tasks in an appropriate manner by ensuring the use of the recommended lifting equipment. Ask for assistance if necessary. Even some propshafts can be difficult to handle.

Propshaft

Jacking and Supporting

Only use the recommended jacking and support points when lifting a vehicle. Refer to the manufacturer's instructions if unsure. Ensure that the jack and support stands, which must be used at all times, have an appropriate safe working load (SWL).

Support point

Skin Contact

When servicing vehicle systems avoid skin contact with new and used engine oils. Use barrier cream or non-porous gloves. Be careful with hot oil, particularly when carrying out oil draining operations. Never keep oily rags in overalls or other pockets and change out of oil-contaminated clothing as soon as reasonably possible.

Wear gloves or use barrier cream

Caution- Attention- Achtung!

All types of fuel and particularly the vapors are highly flammable. They can be ignited from a number of sources. Any naked flame, a short circuit, a cigarette, or, under the right conditions, a hot object will start a fire.

Take care!

Electrical Sparks

The most common cause for fires on vehicles in the workshop is electrical sparks. These can occur during the connection and removal of electrical terminals. Sparks also occur when the engine is cranked with the ignition on and the spark plugs removed. Disconnect the coil or connect the HT leads directly to earth to prevent this.

Sparks from the battery lead

Short Circuits

If a wire or tool is allowed to join the battery positive connection to the negative connection, a serious short circuit will result. A wire would become red hot and in addition to the obvious fire risk, would burn through whatever part of your body was touching it. This demonstration shown here was carried out with trained fire supervision by fully trained experts. Do NOT attempt to copy it. The same results occur if shorts are made on the vehicle. Take care.

Do NOT try this!

Original Equipment

In consideration of other people's property, always be careful to use approved parts. Original equipment manufacturer's (OEM) parts may be required to meet safety regulations.

Use good quality parts[2]

Refrigerant

Refrigerant used in air conditioning systems is dangerous. If it comes in contact with the skin, it produces severe frostbite. Wear protective goggles and gloves at all times. Use gloves designed for the purpose; leather or fabric gloves are NOT suitable. If refrigerant is exposed to naked flames or hot surfaces, it produces toxic gases. Always ensure adequate ventilation when working on air conditioning systems.

Air conditioning system connections

Read the last few pages again and note down FIVE bullet points here:

Pressurized Cooling Systems

If work has to be carried out on the vehicle heater or the cooling system, there is a risk of scalding. The coolant is run at a pressure higher than atmospheric pressure. If the cap is removed when hot, the coolant can boil instantly, ejecting boiling water and steam.

Heater radiator

Rotating Driveline Components

The Ferrari shown here was tested on a rolling road. It was being driven at speeds well in excess of 100 mph! Note how important it is to ensure that all driveline components are in good order.

Ferrari under test on a rolling road

Transmission Wind-Up

On four-wheel drive vehicles, it is possible for the transmission to 'wind up' when the front and rear axles are locked together. This is because the two axles may run at slightly different speeds. When driving on rough ground it is not a problem because the bouncing and movement allows the tires to slip. On hard surfaces, however, a twist or 'wind-up' of components such as driveshafts occurs. When the vehicle is jacked up, the transmission can unwind suddenly causing serious injury. This does not occur on vehicles with an unlocked center differential or a viscous drive.

Simulation of wind-up

Scheduled Servicing

Scheduled service requirements are often quite simple but nonetheless important. Systems should be checked for correct operation. Adjustments, repairs, or replacements are then made if required.

All systems need some maintenance[2]

Non-Routine Work

When carrying out routine maintenance, some non-routine work may be found. This should be reported to the driver or owner of the vehicle before expensive repairs are carried out.

Damaged CV gaiter

Workshop Tasks

Worksheets for routine maintenance of the system are included in this program. Refer to the safety precautions in the health and safety sections before carrying out any practical work on vehicles. The worksheets can be printed and used as part of a practical training program. They give general instructions only, and should therefore be used together with a manufacturer's workshop manual. Other good sources of information will also be required.

Refer to other sources of data as necessary

Worksheet

Service final drive and differential.

Jack up and support the vehicle, or raise it on a hoist. Inspect the area around the final drive and differential unit for oil leaks. If necessary clean off old oil, road test, and check again. Pay particular attention to the main gasket seals and the driveshaft output oil seals and/or the pinion input seal. Remove the filler/level plug and check the oil level. The oil should be level with or just below the threads of the plug. Check with a finger or probe if necessary.

Vehicle on a hoist

Front-Wheel Drive

If topping off is necessary, refer to the manufacturer's specifications for the correct oil. On many front-wheel drive cars, the oil for the final drive and differential is the same as for the main gearbox, because the units are combined. Some vehicles should have the oil changed at certain intervals. If this is the case, drain out the old oil into a tray. It is better to do this after a road test, during which time the oil will become warmer and therefore drain out more easily. Some rear axle, final drive, and differential units do not have a drain plug. In this case, the cover must be removed to drain oil.

Use the correct grade of oil

Rear-Wheel Drive

On rear-wheel drive vehicles with fixed axles and halfshafts, it may be necessary to check for oil leaks into the brake drums on the rear. This would normally be carried out during servicing of the brakes. Refit any plugs and covers that were removed. Lower the vehicle to the ground.

RWD final drive layout

Worksheet

Service 4WD/AWD final drives and differentials.

This operation is similar to the previous task. However, 4WD/AWD vehicles have three differentials and a transfer box. Raise and support the vehicle or use a hoist. Check and top off oil levels in the front gearbox/final drive and/or transfer box and rear differential. Check all seals and gaskets for leaks. Check security and condition of all mountings and drive joints.

Topping off the oil

Read the last few pages again and note down FIVE bullet points here:

Electronic Systems

Some four-wheel drive systems are now electronically controlled. If so, carry out a fault code check of the system. Dedicated test equipment may be required. However, a 'fault memory' warning light will be lit if a problem is stored in memory.

Volvo system[2]

Notes

Regular Checks

Regular servicing is vital for a customer's safety. Carry out checks at all services and report your findings to the customer. Advise customers if anything will need attention before the next scheduled service interval.

Explain any unusual conditions to the customer

Vehicle Condition

Respect your customer's vehicle and take precautions to keep it clean. Repairing or checking some systems is likely to involve you working under the vehicle, and then sitting in the driver's seat. Use seat covers and ensure that the steering wheel is clean when you have finished.

Seat covers in use

Keep Customers Informed

Some customers like to know details of what work has been done to their vehicle – and they have every right to know! This driveshaft gaiter had split, and unfortunately, the CV joint had been damaged due to loss of lubrication and dirt getting in. The customer appreciated having the situation explained.

Customers appreciate being kept informed

Test Drives

Take the customer on a test drive if necessary. It is a useful way of helping them describe problems to you. Alternatively, they could drive and demonstrate what is concerning them. Simple problems like wheel bearing noise can be diagnosed easily this way.

Test drive with the customer if necessary

Shifting

Should a customer express concern about shifting (gear changing), carry out a few simple checks before removing the transmission. With the engine stationary, check that the clutch pedal and gear lever can move freely. Check for correct fitment of mats, rubber gaiters, and sound damping material. Look for play and wear in the gear lever guide and engagement of the shift rod bolt in the universal joint. With the engine running, check for correct clutch disengagement.

Changing gears

Transmission Noises

Should a customer express concern about transmission noises, a few simple checks should be carried out before carrying out any repairs. Check that the outer and inner rubber gaiters and the sound damping material are fitted correctly on the gear lever. Make sure that the transmission is correctly filled with transmission fluid.

Gear change gaiter

Leaks

Should a customer express concern about fluid leaks, the leak must be located before attempting any repairs. Clean the transmission and add some fluorescent additive to the transmission oil. Road test the vehicle and then locate the leak using an ultraviolet lamp.

This oil leak was obvious!

Summary

A customer who is kept informed and treated with respect will return and keep you in a job! Explain things to a customer when asked – it will be appreciated.

Customers will return if they get good service

Read the last few pages again and note down FIVE bullet points here:

Module 4. Checking System Performance
Section 1. Checking the System

Introduction

System performance checks are routine activities that occur during all servicing work. They start at pre-delivery and continue for all scheduled service intervals.

Systems need checking regularly[2]

Quick Checks

Quick checks are quick, but must be thorough, as they are looking for incorrect operation or adjustment and the first signs of deterioration. Detailed diagnostic procedures may be required to identify faulty components. Always refer to the manufacturer's data when necessary.

Manufacturer's data

Workshop Tasks

Worksheets for checking the performance of the system are included in this program. Refer to the safety precautions in the Health and Safety sections before carrying out any practical work on vehicles. The worksheets can be printed and used as part of a practical training program. They give general instructions only, and should therefore be used together with a manufacturer's workshop manual or some other good source of information.

Refer to other sources of data as necessary

Worksheet

Check transmission operation by road testing.

Make a visual inspection as part of the preliminary diagnosis routine prior to the road test; note anything that does not look right. Check tire pressures, but do not adjust them yet (unless excessive). Look for fluid leaks, loose nuts and bolts, and bright spots where components may be rubbing against each other. Check the trunk for unusual loads.

Checking the tires

Road Test Procedure

Establish a route that will be used for all diagnosis road tests. This allows you to get to know what is normal and what is not! The roads selected should have sections that are reasonably smooth as well as other conditions. Road test the vehicle and define the condition by reproducing it several times throughout the road test. During the road test, re-create the conditions described over the next screens.

Road test preparation

Normal Driving Speed

Normal driving speeds of 15 to 50 mph (20 to 80 km/h) With light acceleration, a moaning noise may be heard and possibly a vibration is felt in the front floor pan. It may get worse at a certain engine speed or load.

Road test –
Normal speed

Acceleration/ Deceleration

With slow acceleration and deceleration, a shake is sometimes noticed through the steering wheel seats, front floor pan, front door trim panels, and so on.

Road test –
Acceleration and
deceleration

High Speed

A vibration may be felt in the front floor pan or seats, with no visible shake, but with an accompanying sound or rumble, buzz, hum, drone, or booming noise. Coast with the clutch pedal down or gear lever in neutral and engine idling. If vibration is still evident, it may be related to wheels, tires, front brake discs, wheel hubs, or wheel bearings.

Road test – High speed

Read the last few pages again and note down FIVE bullet points here:

Engine Speed

A vibration may be felt whenever the engine reaches a particular speed. Operating the engine at the problem speed while the vehicle is stationary can duplicate the vibration. It can be caused by any component, from the accessory drive belt to the clutch or torque converter, which turns at engine speed when the vehicle is stopped.

Road test – Normal speeds

Noise and Vibration While Turning

Clicking, popping, or grinding noises may be due to the following:

Damaged CV joint

Loose front wheel driveshaft joint boot clamps

Another component contacting the driveshaft

Worn, damaged, or incorrectly installed wheel bearing

Damaged powertrain/drivetrain mounts

Damaged driveshaft

Worksheet

Workshop task: Checking the viscomatic lock in the rear differential.

Slacken the wheel nuts on one of the rear wheels, and release the handbrake. Jack up the rear of the vehicle and remove the wheel. The front wheels must remain in contact with the ground. Apply a torque wrench to the hub nut and turn the wheel approximately half a turn within one second using the torque wrench. A torque reading of 70 ± 30 Nm should be obtained. Check with the manufacturer's data for specific readings.

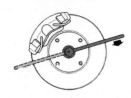

Checking the viscomatic lock[1]

Viscomatic Lock

The free wheel must turn in the opposite direction of the wheel turned with the torque wrench. If the driveshaft turns as well, it must be immobilized. If the specified torque reading is not obtained, the complete viscomatic lock must be changed.

Turning one wheel moves the other in the opposite direction

Summary

Final drive components make a contribution towards safety of the vehicle. System performance checks are therefore important. Cars are used at high speeds and sudden breakdowns can be dangerous. The systems should therefore function correctly at all times.

Busy traffic!

Introduction

Some special test equipment is used when working with driveline components. Remember, you should always refer to the manufacturer's instructions appropriate to the equipment you are using.

Refer to manufacturer's instructions

Dial Test Gauge

A dial test gauge or dial test indicator (DTI) is a useful piece of measuring equipment. It is usually used in conjunction with a magnetic stand. As the needle is moved, the dial uses a series of accurate gears to indicate the distance traveled. The graduations are either hundredths of a millimeter or thousandths of an inch.

DTI and stand[5]

Torque Wrench

A good torque wrench is an essential piece of equipment. Many types are available but all work on a similar principle. Most are set by adjusting a screwed cylinder that forms part of the handle. An important point to remember is that, as with any measuring tool, regular calibration is essential to ensure that it remains accurate.

A torque wrench is a useful tool[5]

Preload Torque Gauge

One type of torque wrench is used to test the turning torque of some components. A good example of this is shown here. The turning torque of the final drive pinion is used to set the pinion bearing preload on some vehicles.

Testing turning torque[1]

Accuracy

To ensure that measuring equipment remains accurate, there are two simple guidelines:

Look after the kit – test equipment thrown on the floor will not be accurate.

Ensure that instruments are calibrated regularly - this means checking them against known-good equipment.

Torque wrench in use

Introduction

The secret with finding faults is to have a good knowledge of the system and to work in a logical way. Use manufacturer's data and recommended procedures. This section includes general faultfinding procedures.

Check data before starting work

Symptoms and Faults

Remember, a symptom is the observed result of a fault. The next few screens each state a common symptom and possible faults. It is important to note that faults in one system can produce symptoms that may appear to be caused by another. Note also that the stated symptoms and faults may vary across different systems.

Symptoms are the result of faults

Knocking Noise

Faults that are possible causes of this symptom are:

Final drive gear tooth broken or excessively worn
UJs worn (not a final drive fault but a common cause)
Bearings breaking up

Check UJs if knocking is the problem

Rumbling or Whining Noise

Faults that are possible causes of this symptom are:

Low oil level
Incorrect preload adjustment
Bearings worn
Worn differential gears

Checking the torque required to move the pinion[1]

Oil Loss

Faults that are possible causes of this symptom are:

Gaskets split
Driveshaft oil seals
Final drive output bearings worn (drive shafts can drop and cause leaks)

Checking the final drive output bearings and seals

Poor Handling

Faults that are possible causes of this symptom are:

Traction control not operating
Limited slip differential not allowing enough slip
Bearings seized

Traction control throttle actuator

Systematic Testing

Working through a logical and planned systematic procedure for testing a system is the only reliable way to diagnose a problem. Use these six stages of fault finding as a guide.

Verify the fault
Collect further information
Evaluate the evidence
Carry out further tests in a logical sequence
Rectify the problem
Check all systems

Stages of faultfinding

Faultfinding Procedure

As an example of how the stages are applied, assume the reported symptom is a humming noise from the rear of the vehicle. Carrying out the procedures outlined over the next five screens would be a recommended method.

Check the latest data

Verify the Fault

Road test the car, with the customer if possible, to check the symptoms. Remember, it is not that you don't believe the customer! It is often difficult for them to describe symptoms without technical knowledge. It is particularly difficult to narrow down sources of noise!

Road test

Collect Further Information

Make sure that you drive the car through a variety of conditions; sharp and long turns in both directions, for example. Drive at low speeds and high speeds. Also, talk to the customer; for example, ask if the noise started suddenly or gradually.

Talk to the customer if possible

Evaluate the Evidence

Remember at this point to stop and think! If the noise has developed slowly, it may suggest a component such as a wheel bearing is wearing out. If the noise is noticeable all the time but worse on cornering, it may help you decide if a wheel bearing is at fault. Alternatively if cornering does not make any difference, the bearings in the final drive or the crown wheel and pinion may be worn.

Stop and think!

Carry out Further Tests

Jack up the car and support it on stands, or use a wheel-free hoist if available. Spin each wheel in turn and listen for noise. Run the vehicle on a wheel-free ramp and listen for noises. Check for oil leaks, as these may be an indicator of other problems. In some cases, removing the propshaft and running the transmission is a useful test.

Driveshaft movement

Rectify the Problem

Once the suspect component has been identified, it must be replaced. Follow manufacturer's instructions for this task. Make sure that the new parts are of good quality.

Crown wheel and differential

Read the last few pages again and note down FIVE bullet points here:

Check All Systems

It is possible, when fixing one fault, to accidentally knock something and cause a new problem. It is also possible that another fault exists, and it may appear to the customer that you have caused it! For both of these reasons, check that ALL systems work correctly when any repairs have been carried out.

Inspect all of the transmission system

Summary

Faultfinding work is rewarding – when you find the fault! Remember to always work in a logical way. The stages of faultfinding can be applied to all systems on the vehicle, complex or simple.

Job finished

Notes

Introduction

Components will usually be removed, inspected, and repaired or replaced when a defect has been diagnosed. Other components are replaced, or stripped and cleaned, at scheduled mileage or time intervals. Refer to the Routine Maintenance section for details on these items.

Good tools and equipment are important

Recommended Procedures

The descriptions provided in this section deal with the components for individual replacement, rather than as a part of other work. Always refer to a workshop manual before starting work. You will also need to look for the recommended procedure, special tools, materials, tightening sequences, and torque settings. Some general and specific tools and pieces of equipment are described on the following screens.

Refer to data as required

General Toolkit

General tools and equipment will be required for most tasks. As your career develops you will build a collection of tools and equipment. Look after your tools and they will look after you!

Snap-on tools[5]

Soft Hammers

These tools allow a hard blow without causing damage. They are ideal for working on driveshafts, gearboxes, and final drive components. Some types are made of special hard plastics whereas some are copper/hide mallets. This type has a copper insert on one side and a hide or leather insert on the other. It is still possible to cause damage, however, so you must still take care!

Some hammers contain metal shot to give a 'dead blow'[5]

Special Turning Tools

This tool is used for turning differential bearing nuts and other similar components. It is, for example, ideal for holding the input flange to a rear wheel drive axle as the main nut is undone. Many workshops have 'home made' versions. Most types are adjustable so they will fit a variety of applications.

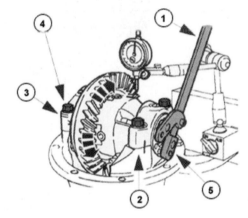

Many special tools of this type are available[1]

Jacks and Stands

Most jacks are simple hydraulic devices. Remember to make sure the safe working load (SWL) is not exceeded. Ensure that any faults with equipment such as this are reported immediately. Axle stands must always be placed under the vehicle supporting the weight – before work is carried out.

Use stands after jacking a vehicle[5]

Ramps and Hoists

Many ramps are available ranging from large four-post wheel-free types to smaller single-post lifts. These large items should be inspected regularly to ensure that they are safe.

Four-post lift in use

Transmission Jack

If a complete gearbox has to be removed, it is likely to be heavy! A transmission jack has attachments that allow you to support the gearbox and lower it safely. The equipment is hydraulically operated, just like an ordinary jack. Often, the height can be set by using a foot pedal that leaves both hands free for positioning the unit.

This jack will support a gearbox[5]

Bearing Puller

Removing some bearings is difficult without a proper puller. For internal bearings, the tool has small legs and feet that hook under the bearing. A threaded section is tightened to pull out the bearing. External pullers hook over the outside of the bearing and a screwed thread is tightened against the shaft.

Internal and external bearing pullers[5]

Air Tools

The whole point of power tools is that they do the work so you don't have to! Air guns produce a 'hammer' action. Because of this, impact sockets should be used. Normal sockets can shatter under this load. It is important to remember that air tools need lubricating from time to time. Air ratchets are very useful for removing or fitting nuts and bolts. However, it is possible to overtighten if care is not taken. Air tools can be very powerful and will trap your hands! Take adequate precautions at all times.

These tools are very useful[5]

Slide Hammer

A slide hammer is a form of puller. It consists of a steel rod over which a heavy mass slides. The mass is 'hammered' against a stop, thus applying a pulling action. The clamp end of the tool can screw either into, or onto, the component. Alternatively, puller legs with feet are used to grip under the sides of the component.

These tools are useful for removing halfshafts[5]

Read the last few pages again and note down FIVE bullet points here:

Grease Gun

A grease gun is a simple device that pumps grease under pressure. A special connector fits onto a grease nipple. Some types are air operated, but the one shown here is a simple pump action type.

Some older UJs can be lubricated[5]

Workshop Tasks

Worksheets for removing, replacing, stripping, and rebuilding the system are included in this program. Refer to the safety precautions in the health and safety sections before carrying out any practical work on vehicles. The worksheets can be printed and used as part of a practical training program. They give general instructions only, and should therefore be used together with a manufacturer's workshop manual or some other good source of information.

Refer to other sources of data as necessary

Worksheet

Remove and refit differential oil seals (FWD).

Raise the front of the vehicle and support it on stands. Place a receptacle under the differential to catch oil when the driveshaft is removed, or alternatively, drain sufficient oil from the gearbox to reduce the level below the differential oil seals.

Differential oil seal in position

Remove Differential Oil Seals

Remove the road wheel, release the tie rod from the steering arm, and disconnect the swivel hub from the front strut. Disengage the driveshaft from the differential and remove the differential oil seal.

Radial lip type oil seal

Refit Differential Oil Seals

Fit a new differential oil seal, with the seal lips towards the differential. Use special press tools as required. Lubricate the seal lips and insert the driveshafts. Connect the swivel hub and tie rod and fit the road wheel. Lower the vehicle, check the gearbox oil level, and top off as necessary.

Removing the seal

Refitting the seal

Worksheet

Remove and refit final drive and differential (FWD & RWD).

Drain the oil from the gearbox and refit the drain plug. Remove the gearbox from the vehicle (this is a separate worksheet). Position the gearbox on its bell housing face and remove the gear case, selector shafts and forks, mainshaft, and countershaft. Lift out the final drive gear and differential assembly.

Draining the gearbox oil

Remove Final Drive – FWD

Remove the roller bearing from the bell housing. Remove the carrier bearings. Remove the differential oil seals. Remove the bolts securing the final drive gear to the differential housing and withdraw the final drive gear. Remove the roll pin securing the differential pinion shaft and remove the pinion shaft. Remove the planet gears, thrust washers and the sun gears. Clean all components and examine for wear and damage.

Final drive assembly

Refit Final Drive – FWD

Fit the pinion roller bearing to the bell housing. Lubricate and fit the sun gears, planet gears, and differential pinion shaft. Ensure that the roll pinhole is aligned with the differential housing and fit a new roll pin. Select a thrust washer, which will provide the correct backlash. Thrust washer dimensions must be equal in both gears. Backlash may be checked using the vehicle driveshaft inner couplings to centralize the sun gears.

Lubricating the sun gears

Final Drive and Differential Assembly

Ensure that the mating faces of the final drive gear and the differential housing are clean and free of burrs. Fit the final drive gear and secure the bolts to the correct torque. Fit the carrier bearings. Fit the final drive and differential assembly to the bell housing.

Gasket surfaces of the final drive assembly must be clean

Read the last few pages again and note down FIVE bullet points here:

Gaskets and Seals

Fit the differential oil seals using special tools as required. Lubricate the seal lips. Fit the gearbox components. Apply sealant to the gear case face and fit the gear case. Fit the gearbox to the vehicle and fill with the correct grade and quantity of oil.

Drain plug and differential oil seal

Remove Final Drive – RWD

Jack up the vehicle and support it on stands. Remove the wheels and then undo and remove the brake drums. Unscrew the bolts holding the bearing clamp and pull out the halfshafts. A slide hammer may be required. Remove the propshaft. Drain oil from the unit if possible – or use a tray to catch the oil as the whole unit is removed. Undo the ring of bolts around the final drive housing. Remove the final drive assembly – with assistance if necessary.

Removing a halfshaft[1]

Refit Final Drive – RWD

Clean off any old gaskets from the mating surfaces. Renew gaskets and use sealant as required. Refit the RWD final drive unit and torque the bolts in sequence. Refit the halfshafts, secure the halfshaft bearings, and fit the drums and wheels. Refit the propshaft. Finally, fill up with the correct oil.

Topping up the final drive oil

Introduction

The main inspections and measurements carried out on the system are included in this section. Inspections should take place at scheduled service intervals, and if problems have been reported.

Inspections and measurements ensure correct operation[2]

Workshop Tasks

Worksheets for inspections and measurement of the system are included in this section. Refer to the safety precautions in the health and safety sections before carrying out any practical work on vehicles. The worksheets can be printed and used as part of a practical training program. They give general instructions only, and should therefore be used together with a manufacturer's workshop manual, or some other good source of information.

Refer to data as required

Worksheet

Inspect and measure differential bevel gears. Note, self-locking differentials are normally factory set and must be changed as a complete unit. Check the specific manufacturer's recommendations. Remove the final drive unit and then strip out the crown wheel and differential. On many systems, halfshaft gears (sun gears) can be examined for excessive play using a feeler gauge.

Checking the freeplay[1]

Halfshaft Gear Freeplay

If the reading is above the recommended value (often about 0.15 mm, but check data), thrust plates must be renewed. Before separating the two halves of the differential, mark their relative positions. Examine all the components for wear and damage. Renew the thrust plates and check that the halfshaft bevels run smoothly. Use Loctite, or similar thread locking material, and tighten the bolts in sequence to the specified torque. Rebuild the final drive unit. Refit to vehicle and top off with oil.

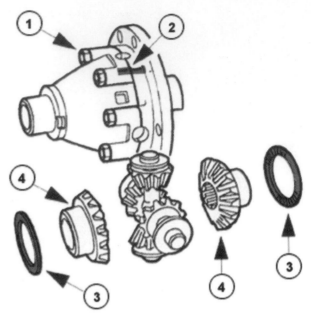

Differential bevel gears and thrust plates[1]

Worksheet

Inspect and measure crown wheel backlash, final drive tooth wear, and pinion turning torque.

Remove the final drive and differential assembly from the vehicle. Note that the figures listed here are typical but always refer to data specific to the vehicle.

Backlash describes the movement of the crown wheel before it contacts and moves the pinion. It is adjusted by setting the position of the two main bearings. Tighten the bearing cap bolts and slacken off again. Then tighten the cap bolts finger tight.

Final drive and differential assembly

Crown Wheel Backlash

Screw the two adjusting nuts, with a special tool if necessary, lightly against the bearings. Set a dial gauge on a magnetic stand and against one tooth of the crown wheel. Tighten the adjusting nut on the crown wheel side until a backlash of 0.01 mm is obtained. Next, preload the bearing on the differential side. Measure the backlash at four opposing points and adjust the nut until a reading of 0.1 to 0.2 mm is obtained. Spin the pinion gear several times, then recheck and tighten the bearing caps to the prescribed torque.

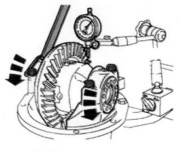

Turning the adjusting nut / Checking the backlash[1]

Tooth Wear Pattern

Coat the crown wheel teeth with touch-up paint or 'engineer's blue.' Spin the drive flange several times while braking the crown wheel with a hardwood wedge. Check the wear pattern and adjust the backlash as required within the specified limits as necessary. Fit lock tabs to the main adjusting nuts.

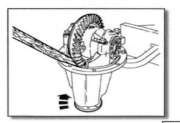

Braking the crown wheel / Ideal contact pattern[1]

Drive Pinion Turning Torque

Measure the drive pinion turning torque using a special torque meter. If the reading is incorrect, a new collapsible spacer must be fitted and the pinion nut torque set. Alternatively, shims are used to set the pinion. Refer to the manufacturer's data for specific instructions. Refit the unit to the vehicle and top off with oil. Use new gaskets as required.

Setting the pinion preload and turning torque[1]

Read the last few pages again and note down FIVE bullet points here:

Summary

Some repairs can involve significant work. However, do not make any compromises. Keep your customers, and yourself, happy and safe.

Job finished![2]

CL

629.
24
ASE

6000 662 132